Kathryn Kuehnle
Leslie Drozd
Editors

Child Custody Litigation: Allegations of Child Sexual Abuse

Child Custody Litigation: Allegations of Child Sexual Abuse has been co-published simultaneously as *Journal of Child Custody*, Volume 2, Number 3 2005.

Pre-publication
REVIEWS,
COMMENTARIES,
EVALUATIONS . . .

"AN ESSENTIAL RESOURCE for those involved in legal cases that include both true and false allegations of child sexual abuse. PSYCHOLOGISTS, CHILD CUSTODY EVALUATORS, OTHER MENTAL HEALTH PROFESSIONALS, AND ATTORNEYS WILL ALL BENEFIT from this thorough review and discussion of issues, controversies, and scientific studies. This book describes appropriate protocols for assessment of allegations of child sexual abuse arising in the context of child custody litigation. It also identifies common mistakes when working with complex issues related to child sexual abuse, child custody evaluation, and assessing for child safety."

Marty Traver, PhD
Clinical and Forensic Psychologist
Columbus, Ohio

More pre-publication
REVIEWS, COMMENTARIES, EVALUATIONS . . .

"IT IS A PLEASURE TO RECOMMEND THIS BOOK. . . . Most helpful to the child custody evaluator in preparing for and presenting the child's needs and the parents' capacities to meet them. An extensive list of references makes this document A VALUABLE TOOL for those who are challenged with such difficult cases."

William L. Bainbridge, PhD, FACFE
Distinguished Research Professor
University of Dayton
President and CEO
ChildCustody.com

"CLEARLY WRITTEN. . . . The text is divided into six sections authored by professionals with expertise about the topic. The reader can benefit from reading the entire book or any one section."

Roslyn Seligman, MD
Associate Professor of Psychiatry
University of Cincinnati College
of Medicine
Distinguished Life Fellow
American Psychiatric Association
Fellow, American Academy
of Child and Adolescent Psychiatry
Diplomate, American Board
of Forensic Medicine

The Haworth Press, Inc.

Child Custody Litigation: Allegations of Child Sexual Abuse

Child Custody Litigation: Allegations of Child Sexual Abuse has been co-published simultaneously as *Journal of Child Custody*, Volume 2, Number 3 2005.

Child Custody Litigation: Allegations of Child Sexual Abuse, edited by Kathryn Kuehnle, PhD, and Leslie Drozd, PhD (Vol. 2, No. 3, 2005). *An invaluable resource for forensic mental health professionals involved with conducting custody evaluations in family court proceedings.*

Psychological Testing in Child Custody Evaluations, edited by James R. Flens, PsyD, and Leslie Drozd, PhD (Vol. 2, No. 1/2, 2005). *"An important new addition to the reference material cited routinely by custody evaluators who recognize the value of staying close to the literature in developing their reports. . . . Provides exciting new empirical findings from Janet Johnston and her colleagues, and gives an insightful view of psychological testing from the perspective of a family law attorney. Newcomers to custody work will be impressed with the breadth of material that this book addresses. . . . Key issues in the emerging science of custody evaluation are discussed." (Daniel J. Rybicki, PsyD, DAPBS, Private Practice, Clinical & Forensic Psychology, Agoura Hills, California)*

Child Custody Litigation: Allegations of Child Sexual Abuse

Kathryn Kuehnle
Leslie Drozd
Editors

Child Custody Litigation: Allegations of Child Sexual Abuse has been co-published simultaneously as *Journal of Child Custody*, Volume 2, Number 3 2005.

The Haworth Press, Inc.

New York • London • Victoria (AU)
www.HaworthPress.com

Child Custody Litigation: Allegations of Child Sexual Abuse has been co-published simultaneously as *Journal of Child Custody*, Volume 2, Number 3 2005.

Cover design by Marylouise E. Doyle

Library of Congress Cataloging-in-Publication Data

Child custody litigation : allegations of child sexual abuse / Kathryn Kuehnle, Leslie Drozd, editors.
     p. cm.
    Co-published simultaneously as Journal of child custody, volume 2, number 3.
    Includes bibliographical references and index.
    ISBN-13: 978-0-7890-3133-4 (hard cover : alk. paper)
    ISBN-10: 0-7890-3133-7 (hard cover : alk. paper)
    ISBN-13: 978-0-7890-3134-1 (soft cover : alk. paper)
    ISBN-10: 0-7890-3134-5 (soft cover : alk. paper)
    1. Custody of children–United States. 2. Child sexual abuse–United States. 3. Evidence, Expert–United States. 4. Forensic psychology–United States. I. Kuehnle, Kathryn. II. Journal of child custody.

KF505.5.C455 2005
346.7301′73–dc22

2005018955

Indexing, Abstracting & Website/Internet Coverage

This section provides you with a list of major indexing & abstracting services and other tools for bibliographic access. That is to say, each service began covering this periodical during the year noted in the right column. Most Websites which are listed below have indicated that they will either post, disseminate, compile, archive, cite or alert their own Website users with research-based content from this work. (This list is as current as the copyright date of this publication.)

*Exact start date to come.

Special Bibliographic Notes related to special journal issues (separates) and indexing/abstracting:

- indexing/abstracting services in this list will also cover material in any "separate" that is co-published simultaneously with Haworth's special thematic journal issue or DocuSerial. Indexing/abstracting usually covers material at the article/chapter level.
- monographic co-editions are intended for either non-subscribers or libraries which intend to purchase a second copy for their circulating collections.
- monographic co-editions are reported to all jobbers/wholesalers/approval plans. The source journal is listed as the "series" to assist the prevention of duplicate purchasing in the same manner utilized for books-in-series.
- to facilitate user/access services all indexing/abstracting services are encouraged to utilize the co-indexing entry note indicated at the bottom of the first page of each article/chapter/contribution.
- this is intended to assist a library user of any reference tool (whether print, electronic, online, or CD-ROM) to locate the monographic version if the library has purchased this version but not a subscription to the source journal.
- individual articles/chapters in any Haworth publication are also available through the Haworth Document Delivery Service (HDDS).

Child Custody Litigation: Allegations of Child Sexual Abuse

CONTENTS

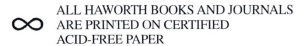

ABOUT THE EDITORS

Kathryn Kuehnle, PhD, received her doctorate from the University of Minnesota and currently holds a faculty position as Assistant Professor at the University of South Florida, Louis de Parte Florida Mental Health Institute, Department of Mental Health Law and Policy. She is a Florida licensed clinical psychologist who also maintains a private practice in Tampa, Florida, where she specializes in the evaluation of children alleged to have been sexually abused and in the treatment of maltreated children and victims of other family violence. She regularly conducts forensic evaluations as the court-appointed evaluator in Family and Dependency Court cases. She further serves as a consultant to the legal and education professions, child protection teams, and other community agencies.

Dr. Kuehnle has published in peer review journals and conducted workshops nationally and internationally on topics related to child maltreatment and family violence. She is the author of the book *Assessing Allegations of Child Sexual Abuse* (Professional Resource Press), which is in its second revision. Dr. Kuehnle also teaches graduate level classes (i.e., Child Maltreatment; Community and Family Violence) at the University of South Florida, conducts annual seminars for doctoral psychology interns on evaluating and treating sexually abused children, and supervises doctoral psychology interns during a six-month Dependency Court internship rotation.

Dr. Kuehnle is the past president of the Florida Psychological Association's Division of Children, Adolescents, and Families; past Ethics chair of the Florida Psychological Association; and was appointed by the Florida Supreme Court Chief Justice to serve as a member of the Family Court Steering Committee. She has been appointed to the Association of Family and Conciliation Courts Child Custody Standards Task Force.

Leslie Drozd, PhD, is a clinical and forensic psychologist. She has an independent practice in Newport Beach, California. She has conducted child custody evaluations for over 15 years and spoken nationally and internationally on issues related to custody, including substance abuse and domestic violence. She is one of the leading experts in the country on domestic violence in child custody cases. Dr. Drozd is author or co-author of many important articles, book chapters, and books including *Domestic Violence: True or False?; Is It Domestic Violence, Alienation and/or Estrangement?; Safety First: Understanding the Impact of Domestic Violence on Children in Child Custody Disputes; What to Do and When to Do It When Children Are Exposed to Domestic Violence; Problems with Attachment in Divorcing Families; Child Placement and Custody Decision-Making in Domestic Violence Families;* and *Hearing the Child's Voice, Supporting the Child's Needs in Child Custody Evaluations.* She is co-author of *The Missing Piece: Solving the Puzzle of Self,* with Claudia Black.

Preface:
Investigating Allegations
of Child Sexual Abuse:
Shortcuts Not Welcome

D. A. Martindale

THE DIVISIONS AMONG US

"We have met the enemy . . . and he is us." It was Pogo, the cartoon inhabitant of the Okefenokee Swamp, who first offered this warning through his creator, Walt Kelly, a nationally syndicated cartoonist. Within the context of this discussion, "we" refers to custody evaluators tackling child sexual abuse allegations. As a group, custody evaluators are eager to assist the judges who must choose among options not one of which provides a neat answer. Among ourselves, however, we are struggling with some very divisive disagreements concerning how best to provide the assistance that courts require.

In 2000, the Honorable Stephen Hjelt wrote what might best be described as an open letter to psychologists. He reminded psychologists that they are representatives of a "profession [with] strong roots as a discipline that has a foundation in the scientific method" (Hjelt, 2000, p. 12). Judge Hjelt reminded experts that their purpose is to assist triers of fact and issued a strong challenge to psychologists. He wrote: "You know in your collective heart that there is much that masquerades as professional psychology that is quackery and sham. Expose it and renounce it" (Hjelt, 2000, p. 13). Judge Hjelt's observations are applicable to all custody evaluators, regardless of the specific professions of which they are members. Not surprisingly, however, those who endorse quackery usually don't see it as such; those who expose it and renounce it are often not well received.

When we meet and air our differences, an uninformed observer listening to the discussion might guess that it had been scripted by Lewis Carroll. With alarming frequency, those who cut corners accuse those who insist on being thorough with being inattentive to the need for expeditious resolution and, by extension, with being less concerned with the well-being of children. This preface is not being written by a dispassionate observer. I acknowledge being an active member of one of the warring camps. I endorse thoroughness, utilization of reliable methods, and professional role delineation.

HOW TO MOST EFFECTIVELY PROTECT CHILDREN

"The court system faces a particularly vexing problem when, in the midst of a custody dispute, one parent alleges that the other is sexually abusing their child. . . . Though providing for the child's safety is essential, neither courts nor mental health professionals have determined how to protect the child from an alleged source of harm without subjecting the child to harm of another type" (Martindale, 2003, p. 178).

We agree among ourselves that children should be protected when there are threats to their physical or emotional health. We disagree with respect to two issues. The first of these is the nature and extent of our obligation to protect the due process rights of those who have been accused of sexual abuse. The second relates to the means by which we can best provide protection to children.

The Presumption of Innocence . . . or Guilt

Associate Justice Anthony Kennedy, in his concurring opinion in *Texas v. Johnson,* 491 US 397 (1989), observed: "The hard fact is that sometimes we must make decisions that we do not like. We make them because they are right, right in the sense that the law and the Constitution, as we see them, compel the result" (at 420-421). Unlike justices of the Supreme Court, evaluators do not take an oath of office; nevertheless, we, too, must respect the law and make a commitment to the process by which allegations are adjudicated. Any one of us has the right to believe that individuals accused of criminal conduct should be deemed guilty unless proven innocent. Any one of us has the right to advocate the abolition of the presumption of innocence. Until such a change occurs, however, it is incumbent upon us to respect the law as it now stands and to presume the innocence of those who proclaim their innocence.

With regard to the thorny issue of providing protection, it must be recognized that termination of the contact between a child and the child's alleged abuser does not necessarily afford protection for the child. When allegations are inaccurate, and child-parent contact is limited to that which occurs between the child and the parent who has registered false or misguided allegations, there is a significant risk that the accused parent who, in reality, is safe will be perceived by the child as dangerous. The long-term implications of this misperception are presumably clear.

Ascertaining Truth

By virtue of the services offered by us, we are obligated to be familiar with the research that clearly documents the inability of psychologists to identify deception in face-to-face interpersonal interactions any more effectively than it can be identified by others (DePaulo, Charlton, Cooper, Lindsay, & Muhlenbruck, 1997; Ekman & O'Sullivan, 1991; Feeley & Young, 1998; Frank & Feeley, 2003). Much harm is done by evaluators who are emotionally invested in protecting children; who are fervent believers in the principle that protection trumps other concerns; and who are profoundly confident in their ability to distinguish the decent from the deceitful. Our inability to discern duplicity is an unfortunate reality that has been established in repeated research studies. It is a reality that must be addressed and that is not altered by the purity of our motives, the fervor of our beliefs, or the strength of our confidence. We are no more successful at identifying the truth telling of the accuser than of the accused.

In an analysis of empirical research findings by Herman (2005), approximately one-fourth of the decisions made by forensic mental health evaluators in cases involving child sex abuse allegations produce either false positive or false negative errors. Kuehnle and Kirkpatrick (this volume) have observed that though "trained forensic mental health evaluators may assist the court by collecting data through forensic interviews, psychological testing, record reviews, and collateral interviews, and by summarizing relevant findings from social science research, it is debated whether forensic evaluators are competent to decide whether or not a CSA allegation is valid. The available data generally indicate that forensic evaluators' substantiation decisions lack adequate psychometric reliability and validity" (Realmuto, Jensen, & Wescoe, 1990; Realmuto & Wescoe, 1992).

Disruption of Parent-Child Relationships

Not all breaks in the continuity of contact between a parent and child produce the same psychological impact on the child. The impact of a disruption caused by a parent's business trip, a parent's hospitalization, and a court-sanctioned suspension of contact the basis for which is the parent's alleged risk to the child are likely to have very different effects upon the child.

The intensity of parental conflict is one of the most significant predictors of children's adjustment to divorce (Kelly, 2000; Kline, Johnston, & Tschann, 1991). A critical element in the child-parent attachment bond is the child's perception of the parent as available, trustworthy, responsive, and protective (Jarvis & Creasey, 1991; Wekerle & Wolfe, 1998). Great damage may be done to a parent-child relationship when one parent treats the other as though s/he is not to be trusted and does not provide a safe environment for the child (Maccoby, Depner, & Mnookin, 1990, p. 157).

If a parent has sexually molested a child, then that parent is neither trustworthy, responsive, nor protective; however, if *no* molestation has occurred, court-mandated separation of the parent from the child creates a significant risk that the child will come to *perceive* that parent as being untrustworthy, unresponsive to the child's needs, and predatory rather than protective. If such a perception develops and if it is inaccurate, it is likely that irreparable harm is done.

SOUND METHODOLOGY: DEALING WITH COGNITIVE BIASES

Diagnostic Suspicion Bias

The presumption that an individual has been exposed to a putative cause (such as sexual abuse) intensifies the search for symptoms, thereby increasing the probability that such symptoms will be observed (Lyon & Koehler, 1998, p. 257).

Equifinality

It is the principle of *equifinality* that explains how several different life events can produce the same constellation of symptoms (Lawlor, 1998, p. 110). For example, Newman (1994, p. 196) has observed that severe headaches are *consistent with* having been hit on the head with a blunt instrument, yet most individuals experiencing severe headaches have not been hit over the head with blunt instruments.

Symptoms viewed by evaluators as evidence of sexual molestation may have developed as a result of life events unrelated to sexual abuse. Consider some views concerning the effects of divorce upon children. "[C]hildren of divorced parents, compared with the children of intact families, are 'at risk' for psychological damage." "[F]amily dissolution and the associated severance of important formative relationships can be damaging to the psychosocial adjustment of young children" (Lamb, 1977, p. 171). "[P]arental conflict entails substantial risk for the development of children" (Wallerstein & Blakeslee, 1989, p. 269).

Confirmatory Bias

The inclination to seek information that will confirm an initially-generated hypothesis and the disinclination to seek information that will disconfirm that hypothesis has been repeatedly documented. This should come as no surprise to us since several well documented psychological dynamics function either to elicit or to support confirmatory bias (Arkes, 1981, 1991; Beattie & Baron, 1988; Borum, Otto, & Golding, 1993; Dailey, 1952; Davies, 2003; Garb, 1994; Haverkamp, 1993; Sandifer, Hordern, & Green, 1970; Skov & Sherman, 1988; and Strohmer, Shivy, & Chiodo, 1990).

When an evaluator commences an evaluation with a belief that abuse has occurred and when the evaluator is determined to secure information from a child concerning that abuse, the research suggests that disclosure of abuse is likely, even if no abuse occurred (Bruck, Ceci, & Hembrook, 1998, 2002; Ceci & Bruck, 1993; Ceci & Friedman, 2000; Ceci, Huffman, Smith, & Loftus, 1994; Ceci, Loftus, Leichtman, & Bruck, 1994; Crossman, Powell, Principe, & Ceci, 2002; Fisher & Whiting, 1998; Mason, 1998). In one high profile case, children were reinforced for disclosure and orally reprimanded for non-recall (Bruck, Ceci et al., 1995). In *State v. Cressey,* 628 A.2d. 696, the court pointed out that "if a child witness sincerely believes that the suggested sexual abuse actually occurred, cross-examination of that child witness may not effectively test the reliability of the child's recollection" (at 701).

A recitation of events offered by a young child is only useful if the recollections offered are provided spontaneously or in response to questions that are non-suggestive and non-coercive and posed by a well-trained, neutral forensic evaluator who is familiar with the cognitive-developmental factors likely to affect the interview process.

Evaluators may inappropriately conclude that a child's reluctance to answer interview questions is indicative of sexual abuse rather than hypothesize that reluctance may be related to a range of factors. A child's reluctance to answer questions related to sexual abuse cannot be viewed as evidence that the child has experienced an event of sexual abuse. If a reluctant child is pressured to answer questions, research demonstrates that young children pressured to provide an answer are more likely to generate *any* answer than to state to an authority figure: "I don't know." [Refer to Poole & White, 1991, 1993.]

The recitation of events in a consistent manner demonstrates nothing when the consistency has been prompted. When one reviews tape recordings of evaluators interviewing children, one may hear evaluators remind children of what they told the evaluator yesterday, followed by a request that the children tell the evaluator "again" what happened to them.

In *State v. Wright*, 775 P.2d 1224 (1989), the Court noted (at 1228): "Once this tainting of memory has occurred, the problem is irredeemable. That memory is, from then on, as real to the child as any other." When the only evidence available to child protection agencies and the judicial system comes in the form of statements from the child's tainted memory, the actions that might bring appropriate punishment to a child molester or vindicate a falsely accused person can no longer be taken.

Evaluators must be mindful of the fact that by the time they become involved in exploring the possibility that a child has been sexually abused, many people with varying degrees of training have probably elicited statements from the child and at least some of those are likely to be people with a vested interest in what the child will ultimately recollect and report (Poole & Lindsay, 2001).

SELECTIVE DATA GATHERING

Data collected within the context of a thorough evaluation increases the probability that we will be able to ascertain what portion of a child's distress might be reasonably accounted for by the high level of conflict between the parents and what portion of the distress can only be explained by examining other potential sources. Unfortunately, the appearance of a particular symptom pattern often increases the intensity of the search for and identification of a putative cause (in the context of this discussion, sexual abuse). This is a manifestation of *exposure suspicion bias.* When sexual abuse is alleged the evaluative task demands that we examine family dynamics, sources of nurturance, each family member's concepts of emotional and physical boundaries, and sources of stress in the child's life, other than sexual abuse, that may support alternative hypotheses to child abuse (Austin, 2000, 2001; Kuehnle, Greenberg, & Gottlieb, 2004).

USE OF PERTINENT DOCUMENTS

Many evaluators review and rely upon police reports and, because of the manner in which the evaluators describe these reports, skeptical readers are led to infer that the evaluators have been seduced by the aura of authenticity that surrounds official documents and/or documents that have been filed by disinterested parties. Trubitt (2005), for example, describes a case in which a mother "alleged spouse abuse and a police report confirmed it" (p. 9). With only rare exceptions, a domestic incident report filed by a police officer is little more than a stenographic record of statements or allegations made by a specific individual to the responding officer. Such a report confirms nothing. Evaluators and those who rely upon their reports must be very cautious in their selection of documents. Particular care is required where statements that appear on official documents are nothing more than statements made by litigants or interested parties. In examining files released by child protection agencies, care must be taken to distinguish statements made by impartial agency staff members and statements taken from others and simply recorded by agency staff members.

ISSUES IN INTERVIEWING

Demand Characteristics

The concept of *demand characteristics* was initially introduced by Martin Orne in 1962 and three of Orne's publications (Orne & Bauer-Manley, 1991; Orne, Dinges, & Orne, 1984; Orne & Wender, 1968) addressed the ways in which demand characteristics in a treatment context might contribute to iatrogenic psychopathology. Broadly defined, demand characteristics are aspects of an interpersonal interaction that tend to cause one of the participants to behave in ways that s/he comes to believe are expected of him or her by the other participant. Orne's concept is also applicable to interviews conducted within the context of child custody evaluations. Reasonably prudent evaluators learn as much as possible from the mistakes of others. The errors made by the State's expert in the Margaret Kelly Michaels trial (*State v. Michaels,* 642 A.2d 1372) have been well documented and have been discussed at length in the professional literature (Bruck & Ceci, 1995; Bruck, Ceci, & Hembrooke, 1998; Ceci & Friedman, 2000; Crossman, Powell, Principe, & Ceci, 2002; and, Fisher & Whiting, 1998).

In its decision in the Michaels case, the court noted that there was a "fairly wide consensus . . . among experts, scholars, and practitioners concerning improper interrogation techniques." "[A]mong the factors that can undermine the neutrality of an interview and create undue suggestiveness are a lack of investigatory independence, the pursuit by the interviewer of a preconceived notion of what has happened to the child, the use of leading questions, and a lack of control for outside influences on the child's statements, such as previous conversations with parents or peers" (at 1377). The Court also noted: "A lack of objectivity also was indicated by the interviewer's failure to pursue any alternative hypothesis . . ." (at 1380).

In the Michaels case, the Supreme Court of the State of New Jersey wisely noted that "[i]f a child's recollection of events has been molded by an interrogation, that influence undermines the reliability of the child's responses as an accurate recollection of actual events" (at 1377).

Disputes concerning the reliability of information obtained by means of interviews with alleged child victims have reached the United States Supreme Court. In *Idaho v. Wright,* 497 U.S. 805 (1990), the U.S. Supreme Court affirmed the view of the Idaho Supreme Court that in light of the known susceptibility of children to suggestive questioning, there were serious questions concerning the reliability of information obtained by an interviewer who used blatantly leading questions, because he commenced his evaluation with a preconceived idea of what the child should be disclosing (at 812-13).

Context Reinstatement vs. Demand Characteristics

It is likely that many evaluators who employ dolls, toys, and other props are unfamiliar with the theoretical basis for such play techniques, but it is the theory of *context reinstatement* (Priestley, Roberts, & Pipe, 1999) that forms the basis for this often-utilized modality. According to context reinstatement theory, toys and other props the characteristics of which are similar to or reminiscent of aspects of the original event(s) may cue the memory (Fisher, Geiselman, & Amador, 1989; Wood & Garven, 2000). Unfortunately, props such as dolls and toys have been found to increase some children's errors. Although props such as dolls may assist older children, younger preschool age children are at increased risk of making errors of commission when asked to use anatomical dolls to describe the genital touching that they experienced (Poole & Lamb, 1998).

Context reinstatement, extensively studied beginning in the late 1970s (Davies & Thomson, 1988; Fisher & Geiselman, 1992; Gibling & Davies, 1988; Memon & Bruce, 1983; Smith, 1979, 1984; 1988; and Smith, Glenberg, & Bjork, 1978), is directly tied to the work of Endel Tulving and his colleagues, which was begun in the early 1970s (Tulving, 1990a, 1990b, 2002; Tulving & Lepage, 2000; Tulving & Schachter, 1990; and, Tulving & Thomson, 1973). It was Tulving who developed the *encoding specificity principle,* which holds that retrieval of a memory is dependent in large part on the stimuli that were present during perception of the event and storage of the memory (encoding) and their similarity to stimuli present during retrieval attempts.

With specific regard to attempts by individuals to recall personal experiences, the encoding specificity principle holds that accurate recollection of an event will be strongly influenced by the similarity (or lack thereof) between salient stimuli processed during the event and the aspects of the event upon which the interviewer focuses. The skillful and well-prepared interviewer obtains as much information as can reasonably be gathered concerning all the event-related elements, some of which might ordinarily be viewed as tangential.

DATA INTEGRATION

Evaluators, particularly those who offer forensic psychological services, are trained in the examination and interpretation of various types of data, including interview data. Both in formal documents providing guidance to evaluators (American Psychological Association, 1994; Committee on Specialty Guidelines for Forensic Evaluators, 1991) and in peer-reviewed articles (Austin & Kirkpatrick, 2004; Heilbrun, 2001; Heilbrun, Warren, & Picarello, 2003; Kanfer, 1990; Kuehnle, 1996; Kuehnle & Reed, 1996; Woody, 2000), evaluators are instructed to consider whether different data are concordant or discrepant.

Interpreting the Data

"[A]n evaluator cannot apply any set of data, whether from a comprehensive evaluation or a risk assessment, to a person who is in a civil proceeding such as a custody suit, with no known sexual offenses in his history, with the determination or implication that those data mean the person is, or is not, a sex offender" (Sachsenmeir, this volume).

Data Suppression

In reading reports prepared by evaluators who have developed a preconceived conclusion prior to data collection, it is not uncommon to encounter skewed presentations of data. Where data supportive of one's position are presented forcefully and where data not supportive of the evaluator's position are withheld; where the recipient of the evaluator's information, perspectives, opinions, and recommendations is a court; where the evaluator knows that the court is utilizing the evaluator's advisory input in order to make decisions concerning issues of visitation and custody; and where the evaluator knows (or, pursuant to applicable standards, reasonably ought to know) that flawed decisions may result in irreparable harm to the family whose dispute is before the court, the withholding of pertinent data and the failure to articulate the significance of discrepancies in data are a profound disservice to the court and the family.

It is noteworthy that because technology makes the alteration of photographic images fairly simple, the National Press Photographers Association includes in its Code of Ethics a declaration that "[i]t is wrong to alter the content of a photograph in any way . . . that deceives the public" (http://www.asne.org/ideas/codes/nppa.htm). Alteration includes selective cropping (as contrasted with cropping done in response to space requirements). The press photographers recognize their obligation to present the whole picture; evaluators must do so as well. Though we use words not images, in our reports and in our testimony evaluators place before courts pictures of the families that have been evaluated. When, in describing the members of a family and the dynamics among them, evaluators neglect to include information that is not supportive of their opinions, evaluators increase the risk that placement and access decisions handed down by courts will be flawed.

The obligation of evaluators to endeavor to resolve discrepancies in data and to report discrepancies when attempts at resolution are not fruitful is so important that some states address this obligation in professional licensing regulations. In New Jersey, for example, the statutes under which the professional practice of psychology is regulated include the following: "A licensee . . . shall not condone distortion, misuse or suppression of psychological findings by the licensee or others" [*N.J.A.C.* 13:42-10.13 (c)]. Failure to report discrepant data constitutes suppression of data.

COMBINING TREATMENT AND EVALUATION

General Issues of Role Delineation

Guideline 7 of the American Psychological Association's *Guidelines for Child Custody Evaluations in Divorce Proceedings* (American Psychological Association, 1994) states: "A psychologist asked to testify regarding a therapy client who is involved in a child custody case is aware of the limitations and possible biases inherent in such a role, and possible impact on the ongoing therapeutic relationship. While the court may require the psychologist to testify as a fact witness regarding factual information he or she became aware of in a professional relationship with a client, that psychologist should generally decline the role of an expert witness who gives a professional opinion regarding custody and visitation issues. . . ."

Though no survey data are available, it is my impression that the vast majority of evaluators recognize that there is an *Irreconcilable conflict between therapeutic and forensic roles* (Greenberg & Shuman, 1997). However, when the APA released the custody guidelines, voices of dissent were heard. Some expressed strong objection to the release by APA of a document the contents of which might "unduly restrict the ability of experienced psychologists to make appropriate clinical decisions" (Saunders, Gindes, Bray, Shellenberger, & Nurse, 1996, p. 34). Saunders et al. also advanced the position that there is no place in an APA document for "[t]he idea that child custody assessors who are psychologists should behave in some idealized, detached role . . ." (1996, p. 33). The reference to an "idealized, detached role" is an allusion to the detachment characteristic of a forensic evaluative endeavor; that is "the skepticism, distance, and objectivity necessary to perform a comprehensive forensic evaluation" (Shapiro, 1988b, p. 84). Saunders and his colleagues make clear their view that a psychologist can function in a helping capacity and, at the same time, offer courts assistance in the adjudication of custody disputes.

Decisions concerning methods are dictated by objectives. A method that may be useful in the pursuit of a therapeutic objective may have unintended and profoundly negative ramifications in a forensic setting, and vice-versa. The importance of differentiating therapeutic tasks from investigative tasks has been clearly established (Clark, 1990; Committee on Specialty Guidelines for Forensic Evaluators, 1991; Greenberg & Shuman, 1997; Lavin & Sales, 1998; Martindale & Gould, 2004; and, Strasburger, Gutheil, & Brodsky, 1997).

TREATMENT REQUIREMENTS

In *State v. Cressey,* 628 A.2d 696 (N.H. 1993), the court declared (at 698) that in order to be admissible, expert psychological evidence cannot rest on a child's account. Unless the expert's testimony is based at least in part on factors beyond and independent of the child's recitation of events, the expert is merely vouching for the credibility of the child's statements. Far too frequently, children are brought to therapists by one parent; allegations of abuse are made against the other parent; the therapist commences treatment of the child; and, ultimately, the therapist appears in court to express opinions based on little evidence beyond the statements elicited from the child.

Treatment issues are being addressed in this article *only* because treatment providers often morph into testifying experts. If the perspective of the *Cressey* court were shared by enough judges, the problems alluded to below would not contaminate the custody dispute resolution process. Sub-standard treatment will always create the risk of harm to those who receive it; however, much of the sub-standard treatment that occurs within the context of custody disputes occurs primarily *because* practitioners are endeavoring to simultaneously function as treatment providers and as experts to the court.

Gathering the Pertinent Data

"In no recognized field of endeavor do professionals act in the absence of an appropriate assessment. Steps are taken to determine the nature and extent of the problem to be addressed and the advantages and disadvantages of various courses of action" (Martindale, 2003, p. 178).

In a discussion of the forensic model, Gould and I offered our perspective on interviewing. Though published research data are not available, it becomes clear during discussions among evaluators that there are differences of opinion concerning the amount of structure to impose upon interviews. It can reasonably be expected, regardless of the structure utilized, that evaluators will formulate appropriate follow-up questions when it is likely that doing so will elicit relevant information (Martindale & Gould, 2004, p. 12). When one reviews contemporaneously-taken interview notes or listens to tape-recorded evaluative sessions, it becomes clear that some evaluators pose questions, write down responses, and fail to pose follow-up questions, even where the need for further inquiry should be obvious.

Though the observations offered by Gould and me appeared within the context of a discussion of evaluations, the same principles apply to pre-treatment interviews. It is professionally irresponsible to embark upon treatment without first having formulated a treatment plan and without having established treatment goals, in consultation with the patient (or parent, when the patient is a child). In order to develop a treatment plan and to set treatment goals, a practitioner must gather and integrate pertinent data.

When we work within a treatment context, the prevailing presumption is that those who appear before us honestly share with us their perceptions of themselves and those with whom they interact. Where children are brought to us by parents, we ordinarily presume that the behaviors, family dynamics, and precipitating events described by the parents are being candidly presented. In a treatment context, we tend to presume that discrepancies between the individual's descriptions and objective reality are attributable, primarily, to the operation of various perception- and memory-distorting phenomena of which the individual is not consciously aware. Only limited thought is given to the possibility of deliberate, calculated lying. Treating practitioners are not trained to be skeptical; skepticism is of critical importance when one parent brings a child for treatment, describes problematic behaviors, and asserts that these behaviors are the result of sexual abuse of the child by the other parent.

Assessing Family Dynamics

When parents are in the process of terminating their marriage, it is likely that each has a different perspective on the history of the relationship, the causes of the disharmony, the precipitating events, the effects upon the child, and what lies ahead for all the members of the family. Under such circumstances, a practitioner cannot assess family dynamics on the basis of one parent's perspective. An accurate assessment of family dynamics, both from a historical perspective and from a current perspective, is critical when a parent brings a child for treatment and asserts that abuse has occurred at the hands of the other parent. Because a multitude of events within a family may cause a child to appear anxious, symptomatic, and sexualized, a child's regressive or negative change in behavior cannot confirm an experience of child sexual abuse. "Life stress as well as such variables as physical abuse and domestic violence are dysregulating to children and reduce their ability to control and inhibit their behavior. Consequently, they are more likely to act out, including acting out sexually" (Freidrich, this volume).

There is no empirical support for the conceptualization of sexual abuse as a stimulus that activates an internal process in the child that is manifested in the form of predictable behavioral and emotional symptoms (Kuehnle, 1998). Just as there are no symptoms which, if observed, constitute clear indications of sexual abuse, there are no symptoms which, if absent, constitute clear evidence that abuse did not occur. Though sexualized play with dolls, excessive or public masturbation, seductive behavior, requests for sexual stimulation from adults or other children, or inappropriate sexual overtures toward other children or adults may be observed in children who have been sexually abused, it is essential that mental health professionals recognize that these behaviors have also been observed in non-abused children (Friedrich, 1990; Friedrich, Grambsch, Broughton, Kulpers, & Beike, 1991; Friedrich, Grambsch, Damon, Hewitt, Koverola, Lang, Wolfe, & Broughton, 1992; and Slusser, 1995).

Behaviors often observed in children who have been sexually abused have been enumerated above. The frequency with which young children whose parents are in the midst of a bitter divorce, punctuated by battles over the child's custodial placement, display such behaviors have been reported by several researchers (Friedrich, 2002; Kelly, 2000; Kline, Johnston, & Tschann, 1991; Lamb, 1977; Maccoby, Depner, and Mnookin, 1990; Wallerstein & Blakeslee, 1989). The prudent practitioner is ever mindful of Ockam's Razor (The Rule of Parsimony), a very loose translation of which is "When you're in Arizona and you hear hoof-beats, think 'horses,' not 'zebras.'"

FORMULATING A TREATMENT PLAN

Though there are many disagreements among mental health professionals with respect to issues of methodology, it is, I believe, generally agreed that treatment is more likely to be successful when clinical interventions are selected based upon the nature of the problems being addressed and when the problems are carefully identified by means of a reasonably thorough assessment process.

One cannot conduct an assessment aimed at determining whether or not a child has been sexually abused, and if so whether the child was traumatized by the abuse, and also simultaneously treat the child for presumed trauma. The practitioner accepting either assignment (treatment provider or evaluator) must be familiar with the many life events that can generate symptoms that are similar to those observed in trauma victims. The family dynamics that typify high conflict divorces and contentious custody disputes, a parent's subordination of a child's needs to the parent's needs, and disruptions in significant attachments can create distress of the type also observed in abused children (McGleughlin, Meyer & Baker, 1999).

When alleged child victims of sexual abuse do not make a disclosure to law enforcement or child welfare personnel and are subsequently placed in treatment in the hopes that disclosure will occur within the treatment context, the therapy often morphs into an extended investigation. The pursuit of appropriate treatment goals related to the contentious divorce and the loss of family becomes subordinated to the investigatory goal. This *investigative therapy* may increase the likelihood of a false disclosure of sexual abuse since young children are at risk to change their stories based on the interviewer's reaction to their statements. If children who are in therapy and who are questioned over many therapy sessions repeatedly state that they have not been abused, the continued questioning may lead the children to believe that they have been providing the wrong answer to the therapist's questions, and the children may ultimately make a disclosure. Often such repetitive questioning by therapists is not documented or is inadequately documented.

No matter what the process is called by the practitioner, if the objective is to elicit information that can be provided to a court, the process is actually an ongoing forensic evaluation and not psychotherapeutic intervention. For this reason, such sessions should be videotaped, so that the therapist's methods and the quantity and quality of the elicited information can be examined. Without clear documentation regarding the therapist's interactions with the child preceding the child's disclosure of sexual abuse to the therapist, the court cannot determine the reliability of the child's disclosure. Where any question exists concerning whether or not sexual abuse has occurred, abuse-specific therapy is contraindicated (Kuehnle, 2005).

DETERMINING VISITATION

When recommendations for supervised visitation between a child and a parent are made by mental health professionals, the reasons for such recommendations must be clarified for the court. Only under the most extraordinary circumstances should such recommendations be made by a child's therapist. Rarely is all the pertinent information available to therapists and, with alarming frequency, children's therapists fail to obtain information from both parents and fail to seek the perspective of both parents.

When a suspension-of-contact recommendation is made by a therapist who has not evaluated both litigating parents, has not collected information that is both quantitatively and qualitatively sufficient (by employing collateral sources and by examining variety of documents), the recommendation should be disregarded by the court. Therapists who make suspension-of-contact recommendations regarding alleged parent-perpetrators and their alleged child victims are exceeding the scope of their education, training, and professional role. They are, in essence, making determinations concerning guilt and innocence. Where there is a reasonable basis for concern that contact between a child and parent may place the child at risk, it is more appropriate that the court order supervised visitation to protect the child from possible future abuse and the parent from possible future inaccurate allegations until a forensic evaluation is conducted.

Even where there has been a finding of fact that a child has been sexually abused, it cannot be presumed that the child has been traumatized. It is not reasonable to presume that any form of sexual contact between a parent and child would, *ipso facto,* be experienced by the child as a trauma. Certain forms of contact–the most obvious of which being some form of penetration–would be painful and typically would be experienced as traumatic, but licking and other forms of contact might be perceived by a young child as pleasurable or as silly rather than as horrible. Where no pain or discomfort is involved, what makes various types of sexual contact traumatic is the *meaning* to the child *and emotional significance* of the act. When a child is too young to understand what has occurred, trauma is not likely to be experienced.

THE ROLE OF THE JUDGE

If attorneys were poured from a mold created by me, motions seeking the exclusion of flawed expert testimony would be filed far more frequently than is now the case. If judges judged as I would wish them to, many of those motions would be honored. Separating facts from flatulence can be more difficult than it might appear and gatekeepers need more training than they are receiving. Currently, much of what makes it through the gate is "quackery and sham" (Hjelt, 2000, p. 13). Courts "may defer too much to the opinion of experts if the subject matter is beyond common knowledge and everyday experience and if the opinion is given with the air of authority that commonly accompanies an expert's testimony" (*State v. Cressey*, 628 A.2d 696, at 698). Effective gate-keeping would bar the admission of testimony offered by treating practitioners in which opinions are expressed concerning sexual abuse and custodial placement.

With increasing frequency, concern has been expressed that evaluators often become *de facto* judges (Eaton, 2004; Hunter, 2005; Schepard, 2005) and that judges fail to examine the bases for opinions expressed by the experts who appear before them [Kozinski, *Daubert v. Merrell Dow Pharmaceuticals, Inc. (on remand)*, 43 F.3d. 1311, at 1315-16; Bazelon, *Washington v. United States*, 390 F.2d. 444, at 447]. Judge Hjelt, presenting a perspective with which no one can disagree, reminds experts and judges that "deference paid to poor testimony logically creates poor judicial outcomes" (Hjelt, 2000, p. 9).

Many judges and many experts would assert that assistance is in the eye of the recipient; that experts should provide that which judges request. I disagree. Just as patients sometimes seek from their physicians treatments and medications that the physicians know to be ineffective and possibly harmful, judges sometimes seek advisory input that may lead them astray. Judge Hjelt has stated with obvious dismay that as he has observed experts and judges dancing together, "it has often been hard to tell who was doing the leading" (Hjelt, 2000, p. 8).

Experts do the leading more often than we would wish to acknowledge (Eaton, 2005). In a thought-provoking article, Thompson (2003) asks: "Are there any rules of evidence in family law?" Thompson is not the only observer of the legal system to note that rules of evidence are often ignored in court proceedings that involve family disputes. Particularly where allegations of child sexual abuse by a parent have been raised within the context of a custodial placement dispute, it is essential that every contact between an evaluator and the child be taped and it is essential that those tapes be preserved. Prior to 2003, space devoted to a plea that evaluators be required to create and preserve detailed records would have been wasteful. In 2003, however, the American Psychological Association (APA) published a text in which the destruction of records is advocated (Benjamin & Gollan, 2003). Benjamin and Gollan have opined that the erasure of tapes made during interviews "prevents the opposing counsel from using contemporaneous material out of context during a later cross-examination at deposition or trial" (p. 35). The Benjamin and Gollan procedure is re-stated toward the end of their text: "All videotapes will be destroyed before the end of the evaluation process . . ." (p. 178).

The intentional or negligent destruction, loss, material alteration or obstruction of evidence that is relevant to litigation constitutes spoliation. In an often-cited New Jersey case [*Prudential Ins. Co. of America Sales Practices Litigation* (N.J.D. 1997) 169 F.R.D. 598], the court declared that "[t]he obligation to preserve documents that are potentially discoverable materials is an affirmative one . . ." (at 615). In *Stevenson v. Union Pacific Railroad Company* (8th Cir. 2004), the Eighth Circuit Court ruled that where there is knowledge of litigation, bad faith intent can be inferred. The definition of spoliation, as it appears in *Black's Law Dictionary* (Nolan & Nolan-Haley, 1990), incorporates the notion that the act of spoliation "constitutes an obstruction of justice" (p. 1401).

When evidence has been destroyed (even if by a court-appointed evaluator, rather than by a partisan), it cannot be presumed that the destruction was innocent. Failure to create appropriate records (such as tape recordings of all contacts with children where allegations of sexual abuse have been raised) or destruction of any portions of a file that has been created while treating or evaluating an alleged child victim is a self-serving act. Failure to create adequate records or preserve and disclose those records makes effective cross-examination impossible. When effective cross-examination is hampered, the risk is increased that errors will go undetected. I presume that we can all agree that evaluators–even those who have been appointed by the court–sometimes err.

CONCLUDING COMMENTS: ALACRITY AND ACCURACY

There are few complex things that can be accomplished quickly and well. Addressing allegations that arise within the context of child custody disputes is not among them. The standards that guide our professional behavior have evolved over time and it is the recognition that certain actions lead to unfortunate outcomes that has served as the stimulus for many existing standards both in the mental health fields and in law. In the mental health professions, we have learned that the use of instruments and procedures that lack reliability and validity are likely to generate erroneous conclusions. We have learned that practitioners who take on two tasks are likely to find that neither has been done well. Standards that admonish evaluators to utilize methods of data collection that are empirically-based and to avoid functioning in dual roles should not be dispensed with when allegations of child sexual abuse are being investigated. In law, the due process provisions have served society well; they should not be ignored in the misguided belief that in doing so, courts will be more responsive to the needs of children.

REFERENCES

American Psychological Association (1994). Guidelines for child custody evaluations in divorce proceedings. *American Psychologist, 49,* 677-680.

Arkes, H. R. (1981). Impediments to accurate clinical judgment and possible ways to minimize their impact. *Journal of Consulting and Clinical Psychology, 49,* 323-330.

Arkes, H. R. (1991). Costs and benefits of judgment errors: Implications for debiasing. *Psychological Bulletin, 110,* 486-498.

Austin, W. G. & Kirkpatrick, H.D. (2004). The investigation component in forensic mental health evaluations: Considerations for parenting time assessments. *Journal of Child Custody, 1, 2,* 23-46.

Austin, W. G. (2000). A forensic model of risk assessment for child custody location law. *Family and Conciliation Courts Review, 38,*186-201.

Austin, W.G. (2001). Partner violence and risk assessment in child custody evaluations. *Family Court Review, 39,* 483-496.

Beattie, J. & Baron, J. (1988). Confirmation and matching biases in hypothesis testing. *Quarterly Journal of Experimental Psychology, 40A,* 269-291.

Benjamin, G. A. H. & Gollan, J. K. (2003). *Family evaluation in custody litigation: Reducing risks of ethical infractions and malpractice.* Washington, DC: American Psychological Association.

Borum, R., Otto, R. K., & Golding, S. (1993). Improving clinical judgment and decision making in forensic evaluation. *Journal of Psychiatry and Law, 21,* 35-76.

Bruck, M. & Ceci, S. J. (1995). Amicus brief for the case of *State of New Jersey v. Michaels* presented by committee of concerned social scientists. *Psychology, Public Policy, and Law, 1,* 242-322.

Bruck, M., Ceci, S. J., & Hembrook, H. (2002). The nature of children's true and false narratives. *Developmental Review, 22,* 520-554.

Bruck, M., Ceci, S. J., & Hembrooke, H. (1998). Reliability and credibility of young children's reports: From research to policy and practice. *American Psychologist, 53:2,* 136-151

Ceci, S. J., & Bruck, M. (1993). Suggestibility of the child witness: A historical review and synthesis. *Psychological Bulletin, 113(3),* 403-439.

Ceci, S.J. and Friedman, R.D. (2000). The Suggestibility of Children: Scientific Research and Legal Implications. *Cornell Law Review, 86,* 33-106.

Ceci, S. J., Huffman, M. L., Smith, E., & Loftus, E. F. (1994). Repeatedly thinking about non-events: Source misattributions among preschoolers. *Consciousness and Cognition, 3,* 388-407.

Ceci, S. J., Loftus, E. F., Leichtman, M., & Bruck, M. (1994). The role of source misattributions in the creation of false beliefs among preschoolers. *International Journal of Clinical and Experimental Hypnosis, 62,* 304-320.

Clark, C.R., (1990). Agreeing to be an expert witness: Considerations of competence and role integrity. *Register Report, 16:2,* 4-6.

Committee on Specialty Guidelines for Forensic Psychologists (1991). Specialty Guidelines for Forensic Psychologists. *Law and Human Behavior, 15:6,* 655-665.

Crossman, A. M., Powell, M. B., Principe, G. F., & Ceci, S. J. (2002). Child testimony in custody cases: A review. *Journal of Forensic Psychology Practice, 2:1,* 1-31.

Dailey, C. A. (1952). The effects of premature conclusions upon the acquisition of understanding of a person. *Journal of Psychology, 33,* 133-152.

Davies, G.M. & Thomson, D.M. (1988). *Memory in Context: Context in Memory.* London: John Wiley & Sons.

Davies, M. F. (2003). Confirmatory bias in the evaluation of personality descriptions: Positive test strategies and output interference. *Journal of Personality and Social Psychology, 85:4,* 746-744.

DePaulo, B. M., Charlton, K., Cooper, H., Lindsay, J. J., & Muhlenbruck, L. (1997). The accuracy-confidence correlation in the detection of deception. *Personality and Social Psychology Review, 1,* 346-357.

Eaton, L. (2004). For arbiters in custody battles: Wide power and little scrutiny. *The New York Times, May 23, 2004,* p. 1.

Ekman, P. & O'Sullivan, M. (1991). Who can catch a liar? *American Psychologist, 46,* 913-920.

Feeley, T. H. & Young, M. J. (1998). Humans as lie detectors: Some more second thoughts. *Communication Quarterly, 46:2,* 109-126.

Fisher, C. B. & Whiting, K. A. (1998). How valid are child sexual abuse validations? Pp. 159-184 in S. J. Ceci & H. Hembrooke, *Expert witnesses in child abuse cases: What can and should be said in court.* Washington, DC: American Psychological Association.

Fisher, R.P. & Geiselman, R.E. (1992). *Memory-enhancing techniques for investigative interviewing.* Springfield, Ill: Charles C. Thomas.

Fisher, R.P., Geiselman, R.E. & Amador, M., (1989). Field test of the Cognitive Interview: Enhancing the recollection of actual victims and witnesses of crime. *Journal of Applied Psychology, 74,* 722-727.

Fivush, R., & Schwarzmueller, A. (1995). Say it once again: Effects of repeated questions on children's event recall. *Journal of Traumatic Stress, 8,* 555-580.

Frank, M. G. & Feeley, T. H. (2003). To catch a liar: Challenges for research in lie detection training. *Journal of Applied Communication Research, 21:3,* 58-75.

Friedrich, W. N. (2002). *Psychological assessment of sexually abused children and their families.* Thousand Oaks, CA: Sage.

Friedrich, W. N. (1993). Sexual behavior in sexually abused children. *Violence Update, 3(5),* 1, 4, 8-11.

Friedrich, W. N. (1990). *Psychotherapy of sexually abused children and their families.* New York: W. W. Norton.

Friedrich W. N., Grambsch, P., Broughton, D., Kuipers, J., & Beilke, R. (1991). Normative sexual behavior in children. *Pediatrics, 88,* 456-464.

Friedrich, W. N., Grambsch, P., Damon, L., Hewitt, S. K., Koverola, C., Lang, R. A., Wolfe, V., & Broughton, D. (1992). Child sexual behavior inventory: Normative and clinical contrasts. *Psychological Assessment, 4,* 303-311.

Garb, H. N. (1994). Cognitive heuristics and biases in personality assessment. In L. Heath, R. S. Tindale, J. Edwards, E. Posavac, F. Bryant, E. Henderson, Y. Suarez-Balcazar, & J Myers (Eds.), *Applications of heuristics and biases to social issues* (pp. 73-90). NY: Plenum.

Gibling, F., & Davies, G.M. (1988). Reinstatement of context following exposure to postevent information. *British Journal of Psychology, 79,* 129-141.

Greenberg, S. A. & Shuman, D. W. (1997). Irreconcilable conflict between therapeutic and forensic roles. *Professional Psychology: Research and Practice, 28:1,* 50-57.

Haverkamp, B. E. (1993). Confirmatory bias in hypothesis testing for client-identified and counselor self-generated hypotheses. *Journal of Counseling Psychology, 40:3,* 303-315.

Heilbrun, K. (2001). *Principles of forensic mental health assessment.* New York: Kluwer Academic/Plenum Publishers.

Heilbrun, K., Warren, J., & Picarello, K. (2003). Third party information in forensic assessment. In A. M. Goldstein (Volume Ed.), I. B. Weiner (Ed. In Chief), *Handbook of psychology: Volume 11, forensic psychology* (pp. 69-86). New York: John Wiley & Sons.

Herman, S. (2005). Improving decision making in forensic child sexual abuse evaluations. *Law and Human Behavior, 29,* 87-120.

Hjelt, S. (2000). Professional psychology: A view from the bench. *Register Report, 26:1,* 8-13.

Hunter, L. (2005). Introduction to the symposium issue on child custody evaluations. *Family Court Review, 43:2,* 191-192.

Jarvis, P.A., & Creasey, G.L. (1991). Parental stress, coping and attachment in families with an 18-month old infant. *Infant Behavior and Development, 14,* 383-395.

Kanfer, R. (1990). Motivation and individual differences in learning: An integration of developmental, differential, and cognitive perspectives. *Learning and Individual Differences, 2,* 219-237.

Kelly, J. B. (2000). Children's adjustment in conflicted marriage and divorce: A decade of research. *Journal of the American Academy of Child and Adolescent Psychiatry, 39,* 963-973.

Kline, M., Johnston, J. R., & Tschann, J. M. (1991). The long shadow of marital conflict: A model of children's postdivorce adjustment. *Journal of Marriage and the Family, 53,* 297-309.

Kobak, R. (1999). The emotional dynamics of disruptions in attachment relationships: Implications for theory, research, and clinical intervention. Pages 21-43 in J. Cassidy & P.R. Shaver (Eds.), *Handbook of attachment*. New York: Guilford.

Kuehnle, K. (2005). Treatment of child sexual abuse. Pages 430-435 in G. P. Koocher, J. C. Norcross, & S. S. Hill, III (Eds.) *Psychologists' Desk Reference*. New York: Oxford.

Kuehnle, K. (1998). Child sexual abuse evaluations: The scientist-practitioner model. *Behavioral Sciences & the Law, 16,* 5-20.

Kuehnle, K. (1996). *Assessing allegations of child sexual abuse*. Sarasota, FL: Professional Resource Press.

Kuehnle, K., Greenberg, L. R., & Gottlieb, M. C. (2004). Incorporating the principles of scientifically based child interviews into family law cases. *Journal of Child Custody, 1(1),* 97-114.

Kuehnle, K., & Reed, R. (1996). Evaluating allegations of child sexual abuse: What are in the best interests of the child. *The Family Law Commentator*. Tallahassee, Fl: Florida Bar.

Lamb, M. E. (1977). The effects of divorce on children's personality development. *Journal of divorce, 1:2,* 163-174.

Lavin, M. & Sales, B. D. (1998). Moral justifications for limits on expert testimony. Pp. 59-84 in S. J. Ceci & H. Hembrooke, *Expert witnesses in child abuse cases: What can and should be said in court*. Washington, DC: American Psychological Association.

Lawlor, R. J. (1998). The expert witness in child sexual abuse cases: A clinician's view. Pp. 105-122 in S. J. Ceci & H. Hembrooke, *Expert witnesses in child abuse cases: What can and should be said in court*. Washington, DC: American Psychological Association.

Lyon, T. D. & Koehler, J. J. (1998). Where researchers fear to tread: Interpretive differences among testifying experts in child sexual abuse cases. Pages 249-264 in S. J. Ceci & H. Hembrooke, *Expert witnesses in child abuse cases: What can and should be said in court*. Washington, DC: American Psychological Association.

Maccoby, E. E., Depner, C. E. & Mnookin, R. H. (1990). Co-parenting in the second year after divorce. *The Journal of Marriage and the Family, 52:1,* 157-170.

Martindale, D. A. (2003). Review of Benjamin & Gollan's "Family evaluation in child custody litigation." *Behavioral Sciences & The Law, 21:4,* 547-557.

Martindale, D. A. & Gould, J. W. (2004). The Forensic Model: Ethics and Scientific Methodology Applied to Custody Evaluations. *Journal of Child Custody, 1:2,* 1-22.

Marvin, R.S., & Britner, P.A. Normative development: The ontogeny of attachment. In J. Cassidy & P.R. Shaver (Eds.), *Handbook of attachment*. New York: Guilford; 1999: 44-67.

Mason, M. A. (1998). Expert testimony regarding the characteristics of sexually abused children: A controversy on both sides of the bench. Pp. 217-236 in S. J. Ceci & H. Hembrooke, *Expert witnesses in child abuse cases: What can and should be said in court*. Washington, DC: American Psychological Association.

McGleughlin, J., Meyer, S. & Baker, J. (1999). Assessing Sexual Abuse Allegations in Divorce, Custody, and Visitation Disputes. Pages 357-388 in Galatzer-Levy, Robert & Kraus, Louis (Eds.). *The Scientific Basis of Child Custody Decisions.* NY: Wiley.

Memon, A., & Bruce, V. (1983). The effects of encoding strategy and context change on face recognition. *Human Learning, 2,* 313-326.

Newman, S. A. (1994). Assessing the quality of expert testimony in cases involving children. *Journal of psychiatry and law, 22,* 181-234

Nolan, J. R. & Nolan-Haley, J. M. (1990). *Black's law dictionary (6th ed.).* St. Paul, MN: West.

Orne, M. T. (1962). On the social psychology of the psychological experiment: With particular reference to demand characteristics and their implications. *American Psychologist, 17,* 776-783.

Orne, M. T., & Bauer-Manley N. K. (1991). Disorders of self: Myths, metaphors, and demand characteristics of treatment. In J. Strauss & G. R. Goethals (Eds.), *The self: Interdisciplinary approaches* (pp. 93-106). New York: Springer-Verlag.

Orne, M. T., & Wender, P. H. (1968). Anticipatory socialization for psychotherapy: Method and rationale. *American Journal of Psychiatry, 124,* 1202-1212.

Orne, M. T., Dinges, D. F., & Orne, E. C. (1984). On the differential diagnosis of multiple personality in the forensic context. *International Journal of Clinical and Experimental Hypnosis, 32,* 118-169.

Poole, D. A., & Lamb, M. E. (1998). *Investigative interviews of children: A guide for helping professionals.* Washington, DC: American Psychological Association.

Poole, D. A., & Lindsay, D. S. (2001). Children's eyewitness reports after exposure to misinformation from parents. *Journal of Experimental Psychology: Applied, 7(1),* 27-50.

Poole, D. A., & White, L. T. (1993). Two years later: Effects of question repetition and retention interval on the eyewitness testimony of children and adults. *Developmental Psychology, 29(5),* 844-853.

Poole, D. A., & White, L. T. (1991). Effects of question repetition on the eyewitness testimony of children & adults. *Developmental Psychology, 27,* 975-986.

Priestley, G., Roberts, S. & Pipe, M. E. (1999). Returning to the scene: Reminders and context reinstatement enhance children's recall. *Developmental Psychology, 35:4,* 1006-1019.

Realmuto, G. M., Jensen, J., & Wescoe, S. (1990). Specificity and sensitivity of sexually anatomically correct dolls in substantiating abuse: A pilot study. *Journal of the American Academy of Child Adolescent Psychiatry, 29,* 743-746.

Realmuto, G. M., & Wescoe, S. (1992). Agreement among professionals about a child's sexual abuse status: Interviews with sexually anatomically correct dolls as indicators of abuse. *Child Abuse and Neglect, 16,* 719-725.

Saywitz, K. J., & Goodman, G. S. (1996). Interviewing children in and out of court: Current research and practical implications. In L. Berliner, J. Briere, & J. Bulkley (Eds.) *APSAC handbook on child maltreatment.* Newbury Park, CA: Sage.

Sandifer, M., Hordern, A., & Green, L. (1970). The psychiatric interview: The impact of the first three minutes. *American Journal of Psychiatry, 126,* 968-973.

Saunders, T. R., Gindes, M., Bray, J. H., Shellenberger, S., & Nurse, A. R. (1996). Should psychotherapists be concerned about the new APA child custody guidelines? *Psychotherapy Bulletin, 31:3,* 28-35.

Shapiro, D. L. (1988b). Ethical constraints in forensic settings: Understanding the limits of our expertise. *Psychotherapy in Private Practice, 6:1,* 71-86.

Schepard, A. (2005). Mental health evaluations in child custody disputes. *Family Court Review, 43:2,* 187-190.

Skov, R. B. & Sherman, S. J. (1988). Information-gathering processes: Diagnosticity, hypothesis-confirmatory strategies, and perceived hypothesis confirmation. *Journal of Experimental Social Psychology, 22,* 93-121.

Slusser, M. M. (1995). Manifestations of sexual abuse in preschool-age children. *Issues in Mental Health Nursing, 16,* 481-491.

Smith, S.M. (1979). Remembering in and out of context. *Journal of Experimental Psychology: Human Learning and Memory, 5,* 460-471.

Smith, S.M. (1984). A comparison of two techniques for reducing context-dependent forgetting. *Memory & Cognition, 12,* 477-482.

Smith, S.M. (1988) Environmental Context-Dependent Memory In G. Davies & D. Thomson (Eds.) *Memory in Context: Context in Memory.* London: Wiley.

Smith, S.M., Glenberg, A., & Bjork, R.A. (1978). Environmental context and human memory. *Memory and Cognition, 6,* 342-353.

Strasburger, L.H., Gutheil, T.G., Brodsky, A. (1997). On wearing two hats: role conflict in serving both as psychotherapist and expert witness. *American Journal of Psychiatry, 154,* 448-456

Strohmer, D.C., Shivy, V. A., & Chiodo, A. L. (1990). Information processing strategies in counselor hypothesis testing: The role of selective memory and expectancy. *Journal of Counseling Psychology, 37,* 465-472.

Thompson, R. (2003). Are there any rules of evidence in family law? *21 Canadian Law Quarterly 245.*

Trubitt, A. (2005). To play or not to play: A response to Martindale, Martin and Austin. *AFCC News, 24:3,* 9.

Tulving, E. (1990a). Encoding operations in memory. In M.W. Eysenck (Ed.), *The Blackwell Dictionary of Cognitive Psychology* (pp. 134-135). Oxford: Blackwell.

Tulving, E. (1990b). Memory systems. In M.W. Eysenck (Ed.), *The Blackwell Dictionary of Cognitive Psychology* (pp. 222-223). Oxford: Blackwell.

Tulving, E. (2002). Episodic Memory: From Mind to Brain, *Annual Review of Psychology, 53,*1-25.

Tulving, E., & Lepage, M. (2000). Where in the brain is awareness of one's past? In D.L. Schacter & E. Scarry (Eds), Memory, brain, and belief. Cambridge, MA: Harvard University Press.

Tulving, E., & Schacter, D.L. (1990). Priming and human memory systems. *Science, 247,* 301-306.

Tulving, E., & Thomson, D.M. (1973). Encoding specificity and retrieval processes in episodic memory. *Psychological Review, 80,* 352-373.

Wallerstein, J. S. & Blakeslee, S. (1989). *Second Chances: Men, women, and children a decade of divorce.* New York: Ticknor & Fields.

Wekerle, C., & Wolfe, D.A. (1998). Windows for preventing child and partner abuse: Early childhood and adolescence. Pages 339-369 in P.K. Trickett & C.S. Schellenbach (Eds.), *Violence against children in the family and the community.* Washington, DC: American Psychological Association.

Wood, J.M., & Garven, S. (2000). How sexual abuse interviews go astray: Implications for prosecutors, police, and child protection services. *Child Maltreatment: Journal of the American Professional Society on the Abuse of Children, 5,* 109-118.

Woody, R. H. (2000). *Child Custody: Practice Standards, Ethical Issues, and Legal Safeguards for Mental Health Professionals.* Sarasota, FL: Professional Resource Press.

Introduction

Kathryn Kuehnle

The *Journal of Child Custody* presents this special issue to discuss the complexities of child custody cases embedded with allegations of child sexual abuse (CSA). Forensic evaluators appointed to assist the court in determining the best interests of the child have the onerous task of assembling the interdependent elements of a child custody evaluation, including the collection and interpretation of data and the communication of results. When an allegation of a child's sexual victimization by a parent is raised as a custody/visitation access issue, the forensic evaluator's task moves beyond the description of each parent's psychological functioning and parenting capacity, attachments between parents and child, the identity and needs of the child, and the parents' abilities to meet those needs. When a CSA accusation accompanies the custody litigation, it becomes the evaluator's task to assist the court in determining the veracity of the allegation and the safety of the child.

When the special issue of alleged CSA accompanies a litigated child custody evaluation, the motives underlying the allegations should be examined. The use of a multiple hypotheses framework and delineation of rival hypotheses can be helpful in analyzing data. This volume will

Kathryn Kuehnle, PhD, maintains a private practice in Tampa, Florida, where she provides forensic and clinical services. She specializes in evaluating and treating child victims of abuse, neglect, and other forms of family violence. She is also Assistant Research Professor at The Louis de la Parte Florida Mental Health Institute, University of South Florida, in the Department of Mental Health Law & Policy.

Address correspondence to: Kathryn Kuehnle, PhD, 19810 Gulf Blvd #6, Indian Shores, FL 33785 (E-mail: kkuehnle@aol.com).

[Haworth co-indexing entry note]: "Introduction." Kuehnle, Kathryn. Co-published simultaneously in *Journal of Child Custody* (The Haworth Press, Inc.) Vol. 2, No. 3, 2005, pp. 1-2; and: *Child Custody Litigation: Allegations of Child Sexual Abuse* (ed: Kathryn Kuehnle, and Leslie Drozd) The Haworth Press, Inc., 2005, pp. 1-2. Single or multiple copies of this article are available for a fee from The Haworth Document Delivery Service [1-800-HAWORTH, 9:00 a.m. - 5:00 p.m. (EST). E-mail address: docdelivery@haworthpress.com].

Available online at http://www.haworthpress.com/web/JCC
doi:10.1300/J190v02n03_01

present information on the organizational structure of a complex child custody evaluation with allegations of CSA, the meaning of sexual behaviors demonstrated by children, description of sex offender assessment instruments and the potential for use of these instruments with unidentified sex offenders, the usefulness of the Rorschach in these complex cases, and observations from the Bench.

The first article by Kuehnle and Kirkpatrick presents the reader with a number of myths regarding the occurrence of CSA and victim characteristics. The authors argue that the foundation of most myths is *conjecture* reported as science. An organizational framework for conducting forensic custody evaluations with allegations of CSA is the main theme of this article.

In the second article, Friedrich reviews empirical studies that examine the relationship of sexual behavior to the variables of sexual abuse, domestic violence, physical abuse, family sexuality, age and gender of the child, child behavior problems, and reporter characteristics. He reminds the reader that correlation is not synonymous with causation. In the next article, Sachsenmaier provides a detailed review of instruments used to evaluate and monitor known sex offenders' sexual behaviors. She describes the basic principles of a sex offender evaluation, and how an evaluation of an alleged, but unknown sex offender, might be structured and the data interrupted. Weiner adds to the review of potential instruments by presenting an article on the use of the Rorschach in custody cases with allegations of CSA.

This volume ends with an article by Behnke and Connell that presents a view from the Bench. This article provides insights in to how evaluators may craft their evaluations and testimony to assist the Court with these complex cases.

Evaluating Allegations
of Child Sexual Abuse
Within Complex Child Custody Cases

Kathryn Kuehnle
H. D. Kirkpatrick

SUMMARY. This article provides a framework for identifying and assembling the interdependent elements of a child custody evaluation with allegations of child sexual abuse. The identification of several myths regarding child sexual abuse (CSA) introduces the subject matter of this article. A forensic evaluation model (Heilbrun, 2001) is then used to organize the custody evaluator's tasks into the following sequential classifications: (a) preparation; (b) data collection; (c) data interpretation; and (d) communication of results. Through this model, the entwined tasks of evaluating the child's needs and the parents' capacities to meet the

Kathryn Kuehnle, PhD, maintains a private practice in Tampa, Florida, where she provides forensic and clinical services. She specializes in evaluating and treating child victims of abuse, neglect, and other forms of family violence. She is also Assistant Research Professor at The Louis de la Parte Florida Mental Health Institute, University of South Florida, in the Department of Mental Health Law & Policy.

H. D. "De" Kirkpatrick, PhD, ABPP, is in private practice in Charlotte, North Carolina, where he provides forensic and clinical services. He holds a Diplomate in forensic psychology.

Address correspondence to: Kathryn Kuehnle, PhD, 19810 Gulf Blvd #6, Indian Shores, FL 33785 (E-mail: kkuehnle@aol.com).

[Haworth co-indexing entry note]: "Evaluating Allegations of Child Sexual Abuse Within Complex Child Custody Cases." Kuehnle, Kathryn, and H. D. Kirkpatrick. Co-published simultaneously in *Journal of Child Custody* (The Haworth Press, Inc.) Vol. 2, No. 3, 2005, pp. 3-39; and: *Child Custody Litigation: Allegations of Child Sexual Abuse* (ed: Kathryn Kuehnle, and Leslie Drozd) The Haworth Press, Inc., 2005, pp. 3-39. Single or multiple copies of this article are available for a fee from The Haworth Document Delivery Service [1-800-HAWORTH, 9:00 a.m. - 5:00 p.m. (EST). E-mail address: docdelivery@haworthpress.com].

child's needs, while simultaneously examining the question of child sexual abuse, are addressed. *[Article copies available for a fee from The Haworth Document Delivery Service: 1-800-HAWORTH. E-mail address: <docdelivery@ haworthpress.com> Website: <http://www.HaworthPress.com> © 2005 by The Haworth Press, Inc. All rights reserved.]*

KEYWORDS. Child custody, forensic evaluations, child sexual abuse, abuse allegations

Child custody and visitation access issues present the mental health professional with one of the most challenging categories of forensic evaluations. Custody and access cases that are further complicated by questions of family violence add another dimension of challenge to conducting these unique forensic assessments. This article describes a process for evaluating the issues of child custody cases (CCC) that are interwoven with questions of child sexual abuse (CSA). Other aspects of family violence that may be raised during child custody evaluations, such as spouse abuse, will not be addressed.

MYTHS

The identification of multiple myths relevant to the interaction of divorce, litigated child custody, and allegations of CSA will provide an introduction to understanding the complexity of child custody evaluations with allegations of CSA (also see Wolfe & Legate, 2003). As in most myths, conjecture is reported as science (e.g., significant and escalating numbers of false CSA claims occur with contested CCC). In discriminating fact from conjecture, CSA statistics in general must be explored before subgroups of this population (e.g., accusations of CSA embedded in litigated child custody disputes) can be addressed.

Myth: Reliable Estimates Exist on the Rate of CSA in the U.S.

It may never be known how many children are actually victims of sexual abuse in the United States (Ceci & Friedman, 2000), or for that matter other parts of the world. In the United States, estimates of CSA cases are primarily based on reports received and investigated by child protection agencies. These national figures include duplicate case reports on some child victims, which inflate the national estimates. Conversely, the national incidence figures do not include the number of cases reported to other types of agencies (e.g., law enforcement), specialized programs (e.g., mental health diversion programs), mandated reporters who do not report specific cases, and those cases undisclosed by child victims. The absence of these cases within the incidence figures deflates the national estimates. Thus, national incidence figures do not provide dependable approximations of the actual occurrence of CSA in this country.

Myth:
Only a Minority of Children Avoid Disclosure of Their Sexual Abuse

The majority of empirical studies do not confirm that only a minority of sexually abused children avoid disclosure. Current research shows low reporting rates during childhood by victims of CSA, although there is one outlier study (Fergusson, Lynskey, & Horwood, 1996) showing a significantly high disclosure rate for victims (for a critical analysis of this outlier study, see London, Bruck, Ceci, & Shuman, 2000). A review of retrospective CSA disclosure studies from 1990 forward concluded that two-thirds of the adults alleging CSA did not make a disclosure during childhood (London et al.). The disclosure rates were similar for studies that specifically recruited adults with childhood histories of CSA and for studies that recruited adults from the general population. Furthermore, findings from studies using sexually abused child subjects were consistent with the retrospective findings showing significant delays in disclosure by the majority of children (Elliott & Briere, 1994; Goodman et al., 1992; Henry, 1997; Sas & Cunningham, 1995).

Empirical findings on the relationship of a victim's age and disclosure are variable for victims abused prior to adolescence but consistent for victims abused during adolescence. Experiencing CSA during adolescence was consistently accompanied by a higher disclosure rate compared to that of school-age children, as reported by the adults in retrospective studies (Everill & Waller, 1995; Kellogg & Hoffman, 1995; Kellogg & Huston, 1995). Adolescents' disclosures were typically made to another teenager. When school-age children disclosed, it was typically to a parent (Lamb & Edgar-Smith, 1994; Tang, 2002).

Myth:
**Coercion/Threats and Fear of Harm Decrease
the Likelihood of Disclosure**

The review of research by London et al. (2005) examined not only
the rate of CSA disclosure during childhood but the characteristics of
abuse that were associated with disclosure. Although a number of experts assert that a substantial percentage of sexually abused children
do not disclose abuse because of the method of coercion used by the
perpetrator and fear of physical harm by the perpetrator (Carnes, 2000;
Summitt, 1983), there is little, if any, empirical evidence to support
these conjectures. Instead, London and her colleagues (2005) found a
lack of support for the hypothesis that threats of harm and injury accom-
panying sexual abuse produce non-disclosures by child victims.
Rather, empirical studies showed either higher disclosure rates associated with incidents that were life threatening and involved physical injury to child victims (Hanson, Resnick, Saunders, Kilpatrick, &
Best, 1999; Kellogg & Hoffman, 1995) or disclosure rates that lacked
any significant relationship to method of coercion and threat of harm
(Lamb & Edgar-Smith, 1994; Roesler & Wind, 1994; Smith et al.,
2000). As noted by London et al., further research is needed to fully understand the threats initiated by perpetrators with their child victims.
When the relationship between threats that were used to secure the
child's nondisclosure (e.g., "Don't tell or else. . . .") was examined, the
few studies that reported threat data did not stipulate whether the measure of "threat" referred to statements or actions during the commission
of the assault to produce physical compliance or to threats used to produce silence.

Myth:
**Substantial Numbers of CSA Victims Recant
After Making a Disclosure**

A number of experts assert that substantial numbers of sexually
abused children recant their abuse (Elliot & Briere, 1994; Lyon, 2002).
There are two distinct reasons for the occurrence of the recantation of a
disclosure: the child is withdrawing (a) a true statement of abuse or (b) a
false allegation of abuse. When examining recantations of disclosures,
although research is limited, several studies found that once children
have made an abuse disclosure, they are likely to maintain their allegations during formal assessments (DeVoe & Faller, 1999; DiPietro,

Runyan, & Fredrickson, 1997). Discrepant cases (in which a child dis-closes before the formal interview but denies at the time of the formal interview) represented a small minority and were found to occur most commonly among very young children (Ghetti, Goodman, & Eisen, 2002; Keary & Fitzpatrick, 1994).

London and her colleagues addressed the flaws in a number of com-monly cited studies that have examined recantation (e.g., Gonzalez, Waterman, Kelly, McCord, & Oliveri, 1993; Sorenson & Snow, 1991) and concluded that although these studies reported the highest rates of recantation, the alleged CSA victims in this research had the least cer-tain diagnoses of sexual abuse compared to other studies (for analyses of these studies, see London et al., 2005).

SHIFTING OF INCIDENCE FIGURES AND FURTHER MYTHS

Although the actual occurrence of CSA is not represented by the na-tional incidence figures, these estimated figures reflect rising and de-scending shifts related to societal trends. During the 1970s when CSA became recognized as a significant societal issue, cases of CSA were nationally acknowledged, procedures for state data collection were im-plemented, and the increase in reported cases was reflected in escalating incidence figures (see Kuehnle, 1996). Laws were enacted to protect CSA victims and the punishments executed were generally more severe for perpetrators of CSA compared to those punishments implemented for other individuals who harmed children. Then during the 1990s, CSA reports declined; analysis of national incidence data showed a 26% de-cline in CSA reports nationally, and a 31% to 40% decline in substanti-ated reports (Finkelhor & Jones, 2004; Jones & Finkelhor, 2001). This eight-year decline has occurred in a majority of states. Research has not resolved whether the statistics reflect, among other factors, an actual de-cline, a change in reporters' behavior, a change in investigators' behav-ior, or policy and program changes in child protection agencies. However, other forms of child maltreatment do not match the decline in sexual abuse cases and the researchers of these national findings specu-late one of the reasons for the decline is the intense focus on and severe punishment for perpetrators of CSA compared to other forms of child maltreatment. Research has not been undertaken to provide empirical evidence for this conjecture. Furthermore, it is unknown whether a similar shift exits for CSA allegations occurring during litigated child custody.

One hypothesis is that CSA allegations associated with litigated child custody are consistent across time because of inflated false allegations, which are unaffected by threats of perpetrator incarceration or mandated reporters. A second hypothesis is that CSA allegations associated with litigated child custody match the national incidence shifts in upward and downward trends. If this second hypothesis could be substantiated, the number of CCC embedded with CSA allegations should have decreased over the past decade.

Myth:
Reliable Estimates Exist on the Rate of Litigated CCC with CSA Allegations

Annually, approximately 1.2 million marriages in the United States end in divorce. It is estimated that these divorces involve over one million children (Children's Defense Fund, 2002; U.S. Dept. of Health & Human Services, 1991). For over two million children, ongoing parental conflict may be a permanent condition (Maccoby & Mnookin, 1992).

The numbers reported above are conjectures and do not represent accurate case statistics derived from empirically sound research. Precise information is not available on the overall national or state percentages of dissolution cases that involve: minor children; divorcing parents unable to agree upon custody and/or visitation arrangements; contested custody cases in which evaluators become involved; or contested CCC that proceed to trial. Data are also lacking on the factors that impact individual state differences.

It has been estimated that approximately one-fourth of divorcing couples with children have significant difficulty legally finalizing their divorce without "extensive litigation" (Johnston & Roseby, 1997), and approximately one-fifth of these families re-litigate custody issues post-divorce. Research by Ahrons (1994) provides support for these estimates, with a finding of 25% of her small sample of divorcing parents repeatedly litigating custody issues. Other studies estimate that 5% to 10% of all divorcing parents participate in repetitive litigation at a high level of conflict (Lamb, Sternberg, & Thompson, 1997). If we use a hypothetical one million children as our annual base rate and assign each one of these million children to a dyad of litigating parents, the data would show that on an annual basis approximately 50,000 to 250,000 divorcing couples litigate over child custody issues.

Although some experts claim that a high percentage of litigated child custody disputes are accompanied by CSA allegations, the available research is too limited to draw empirically based conclusions. Several preliminary studies have found approximately 1% to 2% of contested custody cases involved an allegation of CSA (McIntosh & Prinz, 1993; Thoennes & Tjaden, 1990). Based on the above hypothetical numbers of divorcing couples litigating child custody issues, 1% to 2% of these cases would equal 500 to 2,500 or 1,000 to 5,000 contested CCC involving an allegation of CSA, annually. If the lowest estimate of 500 cases is divided by 50 states, there would be approximately 10 litigated CCC with allegations of CSA per year per state. If the highest estimate of 5,000 cases is divided by 50 states, there would be approximately 100 litigated CCC with allegations of sexual abuse per year per state. Thus, a 1% to 2% estimate appears to be a gross underestimate of the actual occurrence of CSA allegations embedded in contested CCC.

Myth:
Reliable Estimates Exist on the Rate of False CSA Claims in Litigated CCC

Another prevalent myth is that litigated child custody evaluations are associated with high rates of false accusations of CSA. Faller (1991) hypothesized that, proportionally, more false accusations of sexual abuse may be made in the context of divorce than in other situations, and the majority of false allegations are made by adults rather than children. Authorities estimate the rate of false allegations of CSA range from 6% to 8% (Faller, 1991; Jones & McGraw, 1987) for calculated lying, or from 23% to 35% (Ceci & Bruck, 1995) if criteria for false allegations are broadened to include inaccurate memories and false statements associated with suggestive questioning and socially desirable responding, respectively (see Poole & Lamb, 1998).

The percentages reported by authorities such as Faller or Ceci are not based on empirically derived data, but are conjectures that should not be stated as science. There are only a few scientific studies that have investigated the issue of custody evaluations and false CSA allegations. Thoennes and Tjaden (1990) conducted the largest study ($N = 9,000$) of sexual abuse allegations in contested CCC and found 2% involved CSA allegations. Of the cases for which a determination of the veracity of the allegation was available, 50% were substantiated as involving CSA, 33% were unsubstantiated and closed with no finding of sexual abuse, and 17% remained undetermined. The limitations of this empirical data collected by Thoennes and Tjaden include the use of custody evaluators and child protection workers rather than the judicial decision-makers to determine whether sexual abuse occurred.

To date, research has not been designed or implemented to produce reliable data on the percentage of contested CCCs accompanied by false CSA allegations (see Ellis, 2000). In cases of false allegations, clear and convincing evidence that the allegations are false is almost always absent. It is difficult, if not impossible, to prove an indisputable negative (e.g., a particular child was never sexually abused). Because the custody evaluator does not have access to accurate base rates of true and false allegations of CSA occurring in the litigating child custody population, the forensic evaluator should assume an allegation of CSA is as likely to be true as not true.

Myth:
Forensic Evaluators Are Competent
at Identifying False CSA Claims

In a review of the literature, Herman (2005) addressed issues of evaluator competency and provided evidence that many practitioners lack adequate levels of training, knowledge, and skills to perform high quality forensic interviews of children or to adequately describe to legal decision-makers the complexity in distinguishing true from false allegations of sexual abuse (Benedek et al., 1998; Berliner, 1998; Lawlor, 1998; Warren & Marsil, 2002). Although trained forensic mental health evaluators may assist the court by collecting data through forensic interviews, psychological testing, record reviews, and collateral interviews, and by summarizing relevant findings from social science research, it is debated whether forensic evaluators are competent to decide whether or not a CSA allegation is valid. The available data generally indicate that forensic evaluators' substantiation decisions lack adequate psychometric reliability and validity (Realmuto, Jensen, & Wescoe, 1990; Realmuto & Wescoe, 1992). In an analysis of empirical research findings by Herman (2005), approximately one-fourth of CSA decisions made by forensic mental health evaluators involve either false positive or false negative errors. The following sections will address the multifaceted tasks of the forensic evaluator conducting child custody evaluations embedded with CSA allegations.

CLASSIFICATION OF THE EVALUATOR'S TASKS

A forensic evaluation model (Heilbrun, 2001) will be used to organize the custody evaluator's tasks into the following sequential classifications: (a) preparation; (b) data collection; (c) data interpretation; and (d) communication of results. This structure may assist the evaluator to move sequentially through a multitude of complex tasks and avoid ethical pitfalls.

Preparation for the Forensic Evaluation

The first component of any forensic evaluation, including a custodial and access evaluation embedded with an allegation of CSA, is the preparation of attorneys and parties through a written document usually referred to as a *Written Agreement* or *Agreement for Services*. This agreement between the forensic evaluator, attorneys, and parties addresses general topics, such as fees and evaluation procedures, and also delineates the unique issues related to these specific child custody evaluations.

Agreement for services: Issues specific to the CCE with CSA claims. Unlike many other forensic evaluations, distinctive issues should be addressed in the evaluator's service agreement, such as (a) observation of the alleged child victim and alleged parent perpetrator, (b) electronic recording of child interviews, (c) contact with professionals and nonprofessionals who have previously interviewed the alleged victim, (d) access to all professional and nonprofessional documents that may contain information about the alleged sexual abuse, (e) permission to use a computer expert for analysis of computer hard drives, and (f) referral of parties to professional laboratory drug screening facilities. It should be made clear in the service agreement that the evaluator, within the boundaries of the law, will determine what information is relevant and pertinent for him/her to review. This decision will not be made by the parties.

It should also be made clear to the attorneys and parties that before an evaluator can provide summary information to the court, *both* parents must participate in the evaluation when the veracity of an accusation of incest perpetrated by a parent is under investigation and the custody and visitation of the child is to be determined. Furthermore, if the alleged child victim is receiving sexual abuse therapy, the Written Agreement will include an agreement by the attorneys and parties for the discontinuance of therapy until the evaluation is complete and recommendations for therapy are developed from the evaluation findings. Furthermore, any therapy involving the alleged victim should be discontinued throughout the custody evaluation when the child's therapist has opined to the court or attorneys the victim status of the child and/or visitation and custody recommendations, unless this child's status has been determined by a court of law.

Appraisal of the evaluator's competencies and role delineation. The preparation phase is multifaceted and also includes self-appraisal of competencies (also see Martindale, 2005; in press), clear role delineation, and acceptance of a legal court appointment. Concerns about CSA most likely will be identified by the court or the parties via the forensic referral questions, or they may surface during the forensic evaluation (although, in the opinion of the authors, this latter occurrence is rare). Forensic evaluators trained in conducting child custody evaluations may not be competent to perform custody evaluations interwoven with questions of CSA. Prior to accepting a court appointment, the custody evaluator must decide if he or she has the expertise to conduct any or all components of the evaluation. For example, the custody evaluator may decide to conduct: (a) all components of the custody evaluation and allegations of CSA with or without consultation; (b) all components of the custody evaluation and assessment of the alleged child victim, with another expert consulting or conducting the assessment of the alleged sexual offender; (c) all components of the custody evaluation and the assessment of the alleged sexual offender, with another expert consulting or conducting the assessment of the alleged child victim; or (d) the evaluator may decline to take the case altogether.

A custody evaluator may also be presented with the first claim of sexual abuse when the custody evaluation is in progress. Under these circumstances, when the CSA claim is at the identified level for mandated reporting, the evaluator should stop the custody evaluation until the legally identified state authorities are informed, the court is notified, and the evaluator receives further direction from the court. Prior to notifying the court, the evaluator must determine whether he or she is competent to conduct a CSA evaluation embedded within the custody evaluation. The court should be notified about whether the custody evaluator is able to conduct all, some, or none of the components of the CSA evaluation. The custody evaluator's procedure for handling unreported CSA allegations that arise during the evaluation process should be addressed in the custody evaluator's *Agreement for Services*.

Accepting an appointment and seeking consultation is not appropriate if the evaluator has little didactic training or experience in the area of interest to the court (American Psychological Association, 1994, 2002). Although few professionals have expertise in evaluating or treating both child victims of sexual abuse as well as adult perpetrators, forensic evaluators may plunge in and conduct the entire evaluation. The evaluator should contemplate whether the potential for false positive or false negative conclusions may increase by conducting these complicated, multifaceted evaluations as a sole evaluator. Presently, there is little, if any, research to address this possible risk (however, see Herman, 2005).

The ultimate issue: Is it within the custody evaluator's psycho-legal role? Most commonly, the evaluator will receive an appointment to a case in which the CSA allegation already has been reported to the appropriate authorities. In such circumstances, the written motion for court appointment should address the allegation of CSA and identify the questions for which the court seeks assistance. However, there remains intense debate regarding the evaluator's position on accepting an appointment order that directs him/her to answer the ultimate issue (i.e., whether events of CSA actually did or did not occur). The authors of this article support the position that it is not within the psycho-legal role of the evaluator to answer the ultimate issue. The evaluator's role is to assist the court by providing data on the strengths and weaknesses of the allegation, not to determine the truth of the sexual abuse allegation. Authoritative sources have argued that, given the current lack of a reliable scientific foundation for determining the occurrence of CSA following an allegation, it is irresponsible or even unethical for forensic evaluators to offer expert opinions about whether or not abuse has occurred (Fisher, 1995; Melton & Limber, 1989; in Herman, 2005). The authors of this article opine that a written motion for court appointment, which directs the evaluator to answer the ultimate issue on whether events of CSA actually did or did not occur, should be returned to the parties' attorneys for revision of this language.

Data Collection Within the Forensic Evaluation

The second component of any forensic evaluation, including a custodial and access evaluation embedded with an allegation of CSA, is the data collection phase. When custody evaluations include allegations of CSA, experts recommend careful review of the nature, sequence, and circumstances of the allegations (timeline development); multiple interviews of the parties; collection of a thorough psychosocial history from all parties; utilization of a structured interview protocol for the children; and the selection of appropriate psychological testing for the parties and their children (Bow, Quinell, Zaroff, & Assemany, 2002). Tasks of the child custody evaluator should also include the review of all relevant documents, including but not limited to child protection agency records and any audio and/or video records of previous interviews of the alleged victim. Findings of child protection services (e.g., "founded" or "un-founded") should not simply be accepted or dismissed, since some child victims may have inaccurately affirmed an experience of sexual abuse (see Ceci & Friedman, 2000; Garven, Wood, Malpass, & Shaw, 1998, 2000) or denied an actual experience of sexual abuse when questioned by state authorities (see Chaffin, Lawson, Selby, & Wherry, 1997; Lawson & Chaffin, 1992). When a child protection services agency (CPS) has primarily relied on the child's statement, further clarification through the examination of contextual factors surrounding the allegation is clearly reasonable.

Developing hypotheses and creating a conceptual framework. It is imperative that the evaluator have a conceptual framework from which to organize the gathered data (see Kuehnle, 1996). The evaluator can then methodically organize data into hypothetical categories in order to rule out various hypotheses. The following list is an example of a partial range of potential hypotheses: (a) The child is not a victim of sexual abuse, but a sincere, hyper-vigilant parent inaccurately believes her/his child is the victim of sexual abuse; (b) The child is not a victim of sexual abuse but a parent is using the allegation of sexual abuse to manipulate the court system during child custody litigation; (c) The child is a victim of sexual abuse, but due to misguided loyalty will not disclose his/her abuse; (d) The child is not a victim of sexual abuse and is credible, but is estranged from the identified parent perpetrator and has misperceived an innocent or ambiguous interaction; (e) The child is a victim of sexual abuse and is credible (modified from Kuehnle, 1996). This organizing format, which utilizes hypotheses, allows the evaluator to systematically analyze data and upon completion of the evaluation to present information to the court in a clear and logical manner.

Selecting assessment tools. In order for the legal decision-maker to understand the unique personality, temperament, behaviors, thoughts, and needs of the child, the custody evaluator is charged with the task of selecting tools and procedures that will assist the court in understanding the psychological identity of the child. In custody evaluations with allegations of CSA, the evaluator should additionally select assessment tools that will assist the court in its ruling on whether a child is the victim of incest perpetrated by an identified parent.

The variability in the temporal, relational, and behavioral aspects of CSA make it difficult to apply a single assessment standard to the evaluation of the alleged child victim (Fisher & Whiting, 1998). For example, intelligence testing with alleged child victims of sexual abuse would not add incremental validity to the evaluation unless the evaluator had questions about the child's cognitive development and ability to process, retrieve, and communicate information within normative chronological expectations. If an alleged victim is achieving academically at an average or above average level and demonstrates adequate communication skills, intelligence testing may be superfluous. However, when an alleged child victim of sexual abuse is developmentally delayed, the results of intelligence testing may assist the court in understanding the extent of the cognitive limitations and the impact of such limitations on the child's ability to provide the evaluator detailed and sequentially organized narrative information.

Currently, there are no standardized instruments that show sensitivity and specificity to CSA (see Friedrich, this volume), and a standardized assessment battery for all ages and types of alleged sexual abuse victims has not been developed. Although instruments such as the Child Sexual Behavior Inventory (Friedrich, 1997) and the Trauma Symptom Checklist for Children (Briere, 1996) show sensitivity to CSA, these instruments do not show specificity to this experience. For example, in a study that examined 1,114 children between the ages of 2 and 12 (screened for the *absence* of sexual abuse) a variety of measures were used, including the Child Sexual Behavior Inventory–3rd Version, to examine sexual behaviors exhibited by presumably non-sexually abused children (Friedrich, Fisher, Broughton, Houston, & Shafran, 1998). The subjects were found to exhibit a broad range of sexual behaviors, with the identified sexual behaviors related to the child's age, maternal education, family sexuality, family stress, family violence, and hours/week in day care. The relative frequency of sexual behavior in presumably non-sexually abused children was similar to results found in two earlier studies by Friedrich and his colleagues, which reinforce the validity of the 1998 results.

While standardized instruments such as the Child Behavior Checklist (Achenbach, 1991) and the Child Sexual Behavior Inventory (Freidrich, 1997) can assist the evaluator in understanding and comparing the parents' perceptions of the child's behaviors with the perceptions of teachers, nannies, and other providers of the child's care, or while the Trauma Symptom Checklist for Children (Briere, 1996) can assist in understanding the child's psychological functioning and identify potential symptoms of trauma, no standardized instrument can *reliably* distinguish sexually abused from non-sexually abused children. Furthermore, research has not found statistically significant differences in the behaviors of sexually abused versus non-sexually abused children with mediums such as children's sand tray play, doll play, or drawings (see Kuehnle, 1996, 2002). When these mediums are used as props during forensic interviews to show as well as tell what happened, the accuracy of children's statements decrease (see Pipe, Salmon, & Priestley, 2002).

Although there are instruments that have been developed to monitor known sex offenders, instruments have not been developed that *reliably* identify sex offenders from the general population or distinguish incest offenders from non-incestuous sexual offenders. Furthermore, there is a substantial risk for false positive and false negative findings when instruments that are standardized on a population of known sex offenders are utilized to evaluate a potentially unidentified sex offender such as a parent, with no known history of child molestation, alleged to have sexually abused his/her child. Sachsenmaier (this volume) provides a thorough review of standardized instruments used for evaluating identified sex offenders and their potential use with alleged incestuous parents.

The child interview: An introduction. Children utilize both physical and verbal behaviors to communicate information about their needs and inform us of the success or failure of their parents in fulfilling those needs. During a child custody evaluation with or without special issues, a child may also verbally communicate important information, such as family dynamics, sources of nurturance, and each family member's emotional and physical boundaries (e.g., does the child sleep with a parent; is sleeping with the parent associated with factors such as the trauma of divorce, enmeshment with a parent, or sexual abuse). This information from the child adds to what is learned from other sources of data in the evaluation process (i.e., incremental validity) and can provide an important source of validation (i.e., convergent validity) when the information provided by the child is consistent with the information obtained through other methods and sources (Austin, 2000, 2001; Kuehnle, Greenberg, & Gottlieb, 2004).

Prior to conducting interviews with children, evaluators should appreciate a number of aspects related to children's memory for events, including: (a) memory is not a video recording of experiences and the status of information in memory changes over time; (b) memory exits in interacting layers of representation (e.g., autobiographical, episodic, semantic); (c) remembering involves a sequence of steps (i.e., encoding, storage, recall) and failures can occur at any step; (d) not all information enters memory and what does may vary in its availability; and (e) recall will be affected by factors such as language development, source monitoring, and styles of questioning (Baker-Ward & Ornstein, 2002). Furthermore, research indicates that children must possess narrative language abilities at the time of an experience in order to provide a delayed verbal account of the event (Peterson & Rideout, 1998). These findings are supported by the empirical examination of the origins of autobiographical memory, which are found to emerge, generally, between two and a half and three years of age and enable children to remember their experiences over time (Nelson, 1993). Baker-Ward and her colleague assert, "The evaluator's task can never be reduced to simply utilizing the appropriate technique to activate a preserved experience in memory or determining when an individual is telling the truth" (p. 32). Our memories are impacted by narrative language abilities at the time of an experience, distorted by our beliefs and expectations, affected by confusions among related episodes or other experiences, and reshaped by additional information acquired after the fact.

An evaluator inadequately trained to interview children may access unreliable information from children, which may then lead to false negative or false positive conclusions on the occurrence of CSA. Child custody evaluators untrained in conducting forensic child interviews should not attempt to interview alleged victims in complex CCC, or for that matter under any circumstances. As Lamb, Sternberg, and Esplin (1998) observe, ". . . The informativeness of interviews with child victims is strongly influenced by the skill and expertise of the interviewers and . . . skillful interviewers can make children into reliable and invaluable informants" (p. 815); the converse position is also true.

The child interview: Factors affecting a child's narration. In designing a child interview, the evaluator should consider five central factors which are found to strongly affect the witness capacities of children ranging in age from toddler through elementary school-age: (a) children's tendency to be reticent and generally uncommunicative with unfamiliar adults; (b) children's familiarity with being tested by adults (e.g., What is the name of this animal?) but lack of familiarity with adults treating them as sources of information that are unknown by the adult; and compared to adults: (c) children's poorer linguistic skills; (d) very young children's poorer memory for events; and (e) children's tendency to forget information more quickly (Lamb, Sternberg, & Esplin, 1994; Poole & Lindsay, 1998, 2002). Passage of time should also be considered, in that time can affect both memory and suggestibility (Lamb et al., 1998).

Further, children may display comprehension problems based on the following assumptions and social behaviors: (a) children assume that adults' dialogue is sincere and reliable; (b) children perceive adults to be trustworthy conversational partners who would not intentionally deceive them; and (c) children consider adults to be highly credible sources of information who know more than they know (Saywitz & Moan-Hardie, 1994). Children may also acquiesce to adults' leading questions in order to please, avoid anger, or protect themselves from embarrassment.

To minimize these problems, school-age children benefit from instructions on ground rules that address these assumptions and social tendencies prior to beginning the substantive segment of the interview, including instructions to: (a) tell only what happened; (b) admit lack of knowledge rather than to guess; (c) remember the interviewer was not present during the event of focus; (d) correct the interviewer when he/ she misstates the facts; (e) not think they made a mistake if the interviewer asks a question more than once; and (f) tell all the details they can remember, even the ones that they think are unimportant (Reed, 1996). Prior to beginning the substantive segment of the interview, school-age children also benefit from instructions on how to provide narrative reports. Strategies for enhancing children's resistance to suggestibility and developing narrations to open-ended questions are less effective with preschool-age children, especially with children under the age of five (Saywitz, Geiselman, & Bornstein, 1992).

The child interview: Documentation. While there is disagreement among professionals on whether forensic child interviews should be electronically recorded (e.g., audiotape, videotape), there is agreement that electronic recording offers the most accurate method of documenting specific questions and answers, as well as documenting the tone of the interview and the skill of the interviewer. The authors of this article endorse electronic recording because this medium leaves a permanent and accurate record for future professional reviews of the interviewer's questions and the child's responses.

The child interview: Recall and recognition testing. Lamb and his colleagues identified the following five types of questions (referred to as *utterances*) used by forensic interviewers conducting child protection investigations: (a) *Facilitator* is a non-leading evaluator prompt for the child to continue his/her narrative (e.g., reinstatement of the child's previous utterance, and non-suggestive words of encouragement, such as "O.K."); (b) *Invitations* elicit an open-ended response from the child (e.g., questions, statements, or imperatives, such as "And then what happened?"); (c) *Directive Utterances* focus the child's attention on details or aspects of the event that have previously been introduced by the child (the majority are WH-questions, such as "What color was that couch?"; (d) *Option-Posing Utterances* focus the child's attention on aspects of the event that the child has *not* previously introduced (these questions have also been called leading questions in other articles, and include questions such as "Were his clothes on or off?"; "Did he tell you not to tell?"); (e) *Suggestive Utterances* strongly indicate what response the interviewer expects from the child and/or assumes details that have not been mentioned by the child (e.g., "he told you not to tell, didn't he?"); the majority of these questions would be identified by mental health and legal professionals as leading (Lamb, Orbach, Sternberg, Esplin, & Hershkowitz, 2002). Recall testing encompasses the first three categories of the interviewer utterances and recognition testing encompasses the latter two categories.

When adults and children are asked to describe events from free recall (e.g., "Tell me everything that you remember . . ."), their accounts may be incomplete but are likely to be accurate. If children are prompted for more details with free recall prompts (e.g., "Tell me more about that."), they often recall further accurate information. Open-ended prompts (i.e., *Facilitator and Invitations*) encourage children to provide as much relevant information as they remember based on their own experience. A caveat to the benefits of recall testing is that open-ended questions can elicit inaccurate reports if a child has incorporated repeated misinformation into his or her memory (Leichtman & Ceci, 1995). When the interviewer shifts from recall to recognition testing, the probability of error rises significantly. With recognition testing (e.g., *Option-Posing Utterances,* such as "Did his finger touch the inside or outside of your private?"), there is greater pressure for the child to respond to the domain of interest presented by the interviewer, whether or not the child is confident of his/her response.

When interviewers ask numerous specific questions, and the format involves yes-no question pairs (i.e., a yes-no question followed by a request to describe the event: "Did Uncle Joe . . .?"; "Tell me about that."), children's performance can be compromised and their inaccurate narrations may increase (Peterson & Bell, 1996; Peterson & Briggs, 1997; Poole & Lindsay, 1995, 1997, 1998). Repeating closed-ended or specific questions also tends to elicit inconsistency and speculation by children (Poole & White, 1991, 1993). Despite these findings, many interviewers progress prematurely from open-ended to specific questions and rely heavily on specific and yes-no questions (Warren, Woodall, Hunt, &

Perry, 1996; Wood, McClure, & Birch, 1996). Furthermore, research on investigative interviews conducted at sites in the UK, USA, Sweden, and Israel show over half of the information obtained by child protection investigators is elicited from alleged child abuse victims using focused (recognition) questions (see Lamb, Sternberg, & Esplin, 2000).

The child interview: Interview protocols. Studies conducted by Steinberg and her colleagues showed that children trained by forensic interviewers to give narrative responses provided responses that were two and a half times more detailed compared to children who were trained to respond to focused questions (Sternberg et al., 1997; Sternberg, Lamb, Esplin, & Baradaran, 1999). These encouraging findings prompted the development of an interview protocol by the National Institute of Child Health and Human Development (NICHD). The NICHD protocol is a highly structured investigative tool designed to translate empirically based research guidelines into a practical interview instrument for use by forensic interviewers (Lamb, Sternberg, Esplin, Hershkowitz, & Orbach, 1999; Sternberg, Lamb, Esplin, Orbach, & Hershkowitz, 2002). The protocol includes the creation of a supportive interview environment (pre-substantive rapport building), adapting interview practices to children's developmental levels and capacities, preparing children for their task as information providers (teaching communication rules; training children to report event specific episodic memories), maximizing the interviewer's reliance on questions that tap children's free recall memory, using option-posing questions only to obtain essential information at the end of the interview, and eliminating suggestive practices (see Lamb et al., 2002). The interview protocol includes a sequence of nine non-substantive and substantive phases, and uses the widely accepted funnel approach in which interviewers begin with open-ended questions that elicit narrative information; proceed to more direct questions with caution, and then move the interview back to open-ended probes that again elicit narrative information (Lamb et al., 1998). Preliminary findings by Lamb and his colleagues indicate that child protection (CP) interviewers who use the detailed NICHD protocol to assist them, compared to CP interviewers who improvise, retrieve more information using open-ended questions, conduct better organized interviews, follow focused questions with open-ended probes (pairings), and avoid more potentially dangerous interview practices.

Currently, there is no single standardized interview protocol consistently utilized by forensic mental health evaluators to interview alleged child victims of sexual abuse. The NICHD protocol may offer mental health evaluators a tool for decreasing false positive and negative conclusions that are based on poorly conducted interviews.

The child interview: How to do it. The lead author of this article has two diverse sequential structures for interviewing children alleged to have been sexually abused by a parent; the two structures vary according to the alleged incestuous parent's visitation status with the alleged child victim. Within these two macro-interview structures are variations based on the children's chronological age and developmental competency. Children under the age of five years old are typically not appropriate candidates for the sequential interview structures described in the following paragraphs.

The first macro structure is designed for children 5 years and older alleged to have been sexually abused but who have ongoing and loosely structured supervised visitation (e.g., visits monitored by a grandparent) or unsupervised visitation with the alleged incestuous parent. The interview structure for this situation begins with a meeting of the child at the home of each parent, prior to the one-on-one formal forensic interviews with the child regarding the substantive topic. The visits to each parent's house is scheduled closely in time (ideally within the same week), with the individual interviews of the child scheduled soon thereafter.

The visitation supervision guidelines, if any, are adhered to during the home visits; the evaluator is not the "supervisor" of any observed home visit. Detailed written notes are taken throughout the observations. The home visits allow the evaluator, prior to conducting a forensic child interview, to establish rapport with the child at his/her homes, to observe the physical safety of the child's living space, and to acquire information from the child about sleeping, bathing, and privacy. If a child attempts to provide the evaluator positive or negative information about the absent parent in front of the other parent, the evaluator should listen to the child's disclosure but not *facilitate* further information. The evaluator should be mindful that a child in a high-conflict custody dispute may feel compelled to say negative things about the absent parent. However, the majority of children involved in high-conflict divorce do not fabricate that a parent has sexually abused them.

When a child discloses negative information about a parent, the child should be informed the evaluator is interested in the child's information and he/she will have time to discuss those topics when they meet later in the week. Throughout the home visit, the child's spontaneous disclosures about the absent parent's behaviors should be addressed in this manner. The child's disclosures at the home visits are not *facilitated* because the child has not been taught interview rules or been prepared to provide information in a narrative form. Furthermore, the child should not be interviewed on the substantive topic in front of either parent. However, if the child makes a new allegation about child maltreatment that rises to the level of "suspicion," the evaluator must report the allegation to child protection authorities that same day and before any further contact occurs between the alleged perpetrator and child.

Following the home visits, the evaluator then conducts two one-on-one forensic interviews with the child at a facility where the child's interviews can be electronically recorded. It is critical that if electronic equipment is used that the sound system and camera are of professional quality and the child's and interviewer's communication and physical interactions are clearly heard and seen. Children and parents are always informed that they will be video- or audio-taped and once in the interview/observation room they are informed again of the electronic recording.

During the two forensic interviews with the child, the steps in the NICHD protocol are followed. The child is brought to the facility by the alleged non-offending parent for one session, and the next session the child is brought by the alleged incestuous parent (accompanied by the legally identified supervisor). Although brought to the interview by the parents, these adults are not allowed to be present or to observe the child interview in progress. The child's disclosures previously offered during the home visit are elicited through the evaluator's use of *directive utterances* or *initiatives,* which focus the child on the topic he/she brought up at home (e.g., "when I visited you at your mother's house you said . . . [repeat exact words of the child]" and is followed by an invitation, e.g., "Tell me about that."). Family photograph albums may assist the evaluator in asking open-ended questions about family members. Once the child has identified the correct name and relationship of the individual in the photograph, the evaluator may query, "tell me about . . ." and then follow-up with *facilitator, invitations,* or *directive utterance prompts.*

A third step in the interview process is scheduling an observation of the child with each parent. Since both parents are asked to be present on the same day at the observation facility, the parents should be scheduled for different arrival times, and put in different rooms to wait. Neither parent should be put in a waiting room with the child. The parent is observed for one hour with the child; parent and child are always informed that they are being observed and video- or audio-taped. Under any type of court-ordered restricted visitation, the evaluator should not allow the child out of his/her view during the observation of the alleged sexual offender and the child, or out of the view of an adult supervisor when the alleged offender remains at the observation facility. The session is electronically recorded and, preferably, observed by the evaluator through a television monitor or one-way mirror. An observation session may be terminated if the child is threatened, whispered to (to avoid electronic documentation), in physical danger of injury, or if there is any indication of sexualized touching. When the hour of observation between child and parent is completed, the parent is asked to leave the observation room. The child will then immediately be interviewed about his or her session with the parent. This interview with the child also will be electronically recorded. The identical procedure will take place on another day with the child and the other parent.

The parent-child observation creates the opportunity for reliance on open-ended questions and the use of *facilitator, invitations,* or *directive utterance prompts.* For example, the evaluator may begin with an *invitation* prompt, "I was just watching you and your dad, tell me about you and your dad." This situation presents an opportunity to discuss positive and negative events that have occurred in the past between the child and this parent and to explore what the child remembers and what the child has been told about the actions of this parent. Discrepancies between the previous information provided by the child regarding this parent and the observed interactions of the child with the parent are addressed with the child. The interview is never conducted in a confrontational manner.

Next, the child is observed interacting with the second parent in order to assess whether the child will accurately narrate the interactions that took place during the session with the first parent. The child and the second parent (in this example, the mother) are observed and videotaped for thirty minutes. This parent is requested to "Please ask your child about the visit with the other parent." Within the same week, this observation structure is again implemented with the roles of parents one and two reversed.

The second macro interview structure is designed for children 5 years and older, who are temporarily restricted from any visitation with the alleged incestuous parent or who are provided highly structured visitation, such as at a community visitation facility. The authors of this article observe that legal decisions regarding visitation following an allegation of child sexual abuse widely vary and may be arbitrarily determined. Judges need to be aware that if parent-child visitation is blocked for an extended period of time, the attachment of the child and parent may be severely damaged. Since the way children process and make sense out of their sexual abuse has a significant impact on their recovery, judges need to consider that a child who falsely believes that he/she has been sexually abused and permanently "harmed" might show signs of psychological trauma and have issues of trust, possibly similar to the child who has experienced sexual abuse. Although we have no research to support or negate this conjecture, judges must consider the potential "harm" of parent-child separation prior to setting orders of "no contact" when allegations of CSA are raised. There are a multitude of options for protecting a possible victim of sexual abuse other than the temporary severance of the child's relationship with a parent.

Within this second macro interview structure, home visits are not conducted because the child is only available to be observed in one parent's home, rather than in both of the parents' homes. Therefore, this second structure begins with meeting the child at a facility where the child's interview is electronically recorded. The child is brought to two one-hour forensic interviews on separate days by a neutral person; the child is not brought to these interviews by either parent. The steps in the NICHD protocol are followed during the two child interviews.

Ideally, the week following the child interviews the child is scheduled to have sessions with the alleged incestuous parent and alleged non-offending parent. The sequence of steps is identical to the first macro organizational structure (i.e., parent #1–child observation, child interview following observation, and parent #2–child observation discussing child's session with parent #1). The parent-child observation session with the alleged perpetrator includes cases of those children with no contact with an alleged incestuous parent (and the parent has not been found guilty of this crime by a court of law). However, the parent-child observation will not take place if there is *reliable* evidence that the child has been physically injured or experienced life threatening actions (e.g., use of weapons) by the alleged incestuous parent. However, it is unlikely that forensic evaluators will find themselves conducting custody evaluations with such egregious findings of child sexual abuse already reliably established.

The commencement of the alleged incestuous parent and alleged child victim observation should *not* be determined by the child or the child's therapist; this decision needs to be determined, after a review of the case history, by the custody evaluator or another expert appointed by the court. If it is determined by a court appointed expert that the child has complex PTSD and would be further psychologically harmed by a parent-child observation, then the observation should not proceed. Unfortunately, children who do not have contact with a parent can become more fearful of a parent through absence, creating further confusion for the evaluator in understanding the CSA allegations and children's symptoms.

It is imperative that the custody evaluator not make a "blind acceptance" that a visit between the alleged perpetrator and the alleged victim will be harmful or "re-traumatizing" to the child. Since it is the evaluator's job to assess the allegations from a multi-hypothetical perspective, the acceptance of such reasoning for *not* conducting the observation/interview may imply acceptance that the abuse did in fact occur. If the evaluator does not observe the alleged parent perpetrator and child victim interacting, the evaluator should specify in writing and document with data the reasons this observation was not conducted. In some cases of CSA or alienation, the child will refuse to participate in a session with a parent. In these cases, the use of a neutral family friend may increase the child's comfort level and compliance. If this supportive person is utilized, it is important to use this person during the parent-child observation session of both parents.

Other observations of parent and child. Observations of the child during individual sessions with the evaluator or during parent-child interactions structured around an activity, such as the family eating a meal or the parent teaching the child a skill, can assist the evaluator in gaining insight into the child's personality characteristics, social skills, boundaries, comfort level with a parent, and responsiveness to structure imposed by authority figures, but may not assist the evaluator in extricating the facts of the allegation of sexual abuse. Parent-child relationship problems associated with child estrangement, alignment, alienation, or abuse may not be differentiated by simply observing children and parents interact (see Kuehnle, 1996 for discussion).

Prior to conducting a parent-child observation, the evaluator should define the objectives of the observation. Research on parenting skills may assist the evaluator in identifying observation objectives, such as the demonstration of positive parenting skills for different age groups of children or parenting behaviors that are associated with children's alienation or estrangement from a parent. There are several possible scenarios associated with why a child may resist contact with a parent, including: a combination of denigration by one parent coupled with poor parenting by the other parent, child abuse perpetrated by one parent, or modeling of fear and hatred by one parent toward the other parent. Children may exhibit relationship problems with parents who lack sensitive parenting skills and who repeatedly push children to engage in tasks that they lack the developmental competency to master successfully. Furthermore, individuals who engage children in sex may become a conditioned aversive stimulus to the child, especially if the sexual abuse involves violence or physical pain. These dynamics may explain all or part of the child's reluctance to interact with a parent. Conversely, the alleged non-offending parent who repeatedly denigrates the other parent in the presence of the child may shape the child's negative image of the other parent. Further, a parent who models fear of the other parent may shape a similar fear response in his/her child.

It can be useful for the evaluator to compare the parent's and child's behaviors at an observed reunion session with historical home video-tapes of the identified parent and child. Collateral reports of the child's behavior with the alleged parent perpetrator immediately prior to separation and blocked visitation may also assist the evaluator in understanding the dynamics of this parent-child relationship, and possibly provide some insight into the dynamics of the allegations.

Collateral sources. It is important for the evaluator to gain access to knowledgeable third parties and review various documents that may provide valuable information regarding the current allegation and any history of previous CSA allegations of the parties' children (Austin & Kirkpatrick, 2004). Evaluating an allegation of CSA is predicated upon information from collaterals, formal documents, and public records.

In contrast to conducting the custody evaluation without special issues, complex custody evaluations embedded with accusations of CSA require a careful review of law enforcement and child welfare records. Among other documents, the evaluator should review electronic recordings or handwritten documentation of previous forensic or clinical interviews of the alleged child victim. Police, sheriff, or child welfare reports regarding the current or previous allegations of CSA and medical records, including but not limited to pediatric records and child protection team examinations, should also be reviewed (Gould, 1998). Documents regarding previously founded or unfounded abuse allegations on other children of the parents, stepparents, or paramours should be pursued.

Interpretation of the Obtained Data

The third component of the forensic evaluation model is *data interpretation* (Heilbrun, 2001). When allegations of CSA occur in a custody case, the evaluator should be familiar with research on children of divorce; CSA; children's normative behavior within developmental stages; the family's culture and religious beliefs; and the potential interpersonal traumatic effects of CSA on the physical and psychological development of the child. As Kuehnle and Sparta (in press) advise, evaluators should never assume cause and effect associations between a single aspect of behavior and the occurrence or nonoccurrence of sexual abuse, nor rely on subjective assessment of the child's "credibility." The evaluator relies on an extensive web of information when assisting the court in determining the veracity of the abuse allegation within the context of custody decisions.

Specialized competence in child psychopathology is essential to distinguish between general developmental functioning and the potential traumatic effects of sexual abuse, divorce, alienation, or estrangement. The evaluator should be familiar with trauma-related symptomatology and understand how CSA, high-conflict divorce, psychological exploitation by a parent, or loss of a parent can alter the progress of a child's development (e.g., attachments, relationships, self-identity, or social and emotional growth). Because there can be significant overlap in symptoms exhibited by children in high-conflict child custody cases and children who have been sexually abused (McGleughlin, Meyer, & Baker, 1999), a parent and/or third party collateral source may confuse the child's symptoms of stress and anxiety associated with the parents' divorce or other traumatic events as symptoms of trauma they believe to be indicative of CSA. It is essential that the evaluator understand the accusing parent's interpretation of the alleged child victim's behaviors. A common error of mental health professionals and lay persons involves the confusion of correlation with causation.

Identifying the meaning of children's behavior. Similar to children's experience of divorce, the experience of sexual abuse does not result in a single symptom or cluster of symptoms that define a syndrome. The view of sexual abuse as a trigger that sets off an internal process in the child that surfaces as predictable behavioral and emotional symptoms does not have an empirically based foundation. When sexual abuse is conceptualized as a single clinical syndrome, parents and mental health professionals may inappropriately identify behaviors and symptoms to support their identification and placement of a child in a fictional homogenous group labeled "sexually abused children" (Kuehnle, 1998a).

Unlike symptom patterns of some psychiatric disorders, the potential symptoms that sexually abused children may exhibit vary widely, and a significant number of child victims may be asymptomatic (Kendall-Tackett, Williams, & Finkelhor, 1993; Kuehnle, 1998c). The broad range of behaviors exhibited by child victims is associated with personality differences, personal interpretation of the event, identity of the perpetrator, characteristics of the sexual acts, co-occurring forms of family violence, family stability, and the parent's response following disclosure. One of the most important findings from research addressing the effects of CSA is that no single sign or symptom, including sexualized behavior (see Friedrich, this volume), characterizes the majority of sexually abused children, a finding well supported from the last twenty years of research (Hagen, 2003). Gratz and Orsillo (2003) reviewed the existing literature on CSA and concluded no accurate and ethical way exists to testify that sexual abuse has occurred based on a child's post-abuse functioning.

When children demonstrate externalizing behaviors, including temper tantrums, defiance, and noncompliance, the custody evaluator should assess if the source of the behavior problems is due to events or actions, such as CSA, alienation, and/or poor parenting skills. Good parenting is found to be critical to the adjustment of the child, and can moderate the impact of divorce as well as sexual abuse (Amato & Keith, 1991a, 1991b; Johnston, 2005). Johnston found divorced mothers who were effective and successful parents exhibited the following characteristics: (a) warmth; (b) authoritative discipline; (c) appropriate expectations; (d) academic skill encouragement; and (e) monitoring of children's activities. Divorced fathers who were effective and successful parents and who reduced the risk of their children's adjustment problems exhibited the following characteristics: (a) authoritative discipline; (b) active involvement in projects; (c) emotional support; (d) involvement in school; and (e) monitoring of activities. Johnston's findings are consistent with Baumrind's (1989, 1991) research, which showed parents from the general population who used a parenting style involving both high demandingness and high responsiveness (referred to as an *Authoritative-Reciprocal* style) tended to have the highest rates of successfully adjusted children. Teasing apart the effects on the child of poor parenting, mental illness, spouse abuse, substance abuse, and sexual abuse remains a daunting task because of the possible occurrence and interaction of these conditions.

Within the last decade, empirical studies have found that in high-conflict divorce, many parents engage in indoctrinating behaviors but only a small proportion of children become alienated (Johnston, 1993). Hence, alienating behavior by a parent is neither a sufficient nor a necessary condition for a child to become alienated. As noted by Johnston (2005), it is critical to differentiate the abused child (who persistently refuses and rejects visitation because of reasonable fears) from the alienated child (who persistently refuses and rejects visitation because of unreasonable negative views and feelings), or from other children who may resist contact with a parent for a variety of developmentally normal and realistic reasons (e.g., the preschooler's fear of sleeping at a new second home). There are a number of reasons that children resist visitation, and only in very specific circumstances is this behavior based on alienation or sexual abuse. Kelly and Johnston (2001) identify children's resistance as possibly being: (a) rooted in a normal developmental processes (e.g., normal separation anxieties in the very young child); (b) embedded primarily in the high-conflict marriage and divorce (e.g., fear, or inability to cope with the high-conflict transition); (c) in response to a parent's parenting style (e.g., rigidity, anger, or insensitivity to the child); (d) arising from the child's concern about an emotionally fragile custodial parent (e.g., fear of leaving this parent alone); or (e) arising from the remarriage of a parent (e.g., behaviors of the parent or stepparent which alter willingness to visit).

As previously identified, problems in the relationship between a child and the parent typically are not the result of a single factor (e.g., alienating parent) contaminating the vulnerable child, but an outcome of the interaction effects of multiple factors (Drozd & Olesen, 2004; Johnston & Kelly, 2004; Kelly & Johnston, 2001). Among these factors are the personality characteristics and behaviors of the aligned or rejected parent, and the child. For example, a child's vulnerability to alienation increases when the child is found to have greater psychological adjustment problems (Johnston, 1993, 2005).

The child's rejection of a parent may be multi-determined by various combinations of the following factors: (a) alienating behavior by the aligned parent; (b) role reversal and separation anxieties between the child and aligned parent; (c) lack of warm-involved parenting by the rejected parent; and (d) critical incidents of child abuse perpetrated by the rejected parent (Johnston, 2005). Johnston's research also found that male perpetrators of domestic violence were more likely to attempt to alienate their children from the victim-mothers, than were the abused mothers.

The final component of Heilbrun's forensic model will be addressed in the next section. This last evaluation component addresses the communication of the evaluation results to the court.

COMMUNICATION OF RESULTS

The fourth component of the forensic evaluation model is *communication of results* (Heilbrun, 2001). During this final step, the evaluator's role is to assist the court in understanding the family dynamics, each party's strengths and weaknesses as a parent, the psychological best interests of the child, and the meaning of the sexual abuse allegation. The results should be described in a coherent and detailed manner and include a description of each parent's psychological functioning, internalization of emotional control, parenting capacity, attachment to the child, and ability to meet the needs of the child. The evaluation should also describe in detail the identity of the child; the unique needs of the child and if those needs are being met by either parent. In CCCs with accusations of CSA, multiple hypotheses may be identified and used to organize the obtained data. When crafting the written evaluation or in giving sworn testimony, the mental health expert should delineate the various possible explanations regarding the CSA allegations and the weight to be accorded to a child's statements and behaviors. This can be accomplished through the generation of multiple hypotheses and the presentation of data that support or weaken a given premise (see Kuehnle, 1996). Using this approach, professionals are able to provide information to the court about the complexity and limitations of our current state of knowledge on CSA while discussing the specific case before the court. When the data that support or negate the various hypotheses are presented in a clear, cogent, and convincing manner, such an approach gives the legal decision-maker a useful perspective on the allegations.

Evaluation results should clarify the dynamics of the relationship between each parent and the child, and how the nature of these parent-child relationships may influence the meaning of the sexual abuse allegation. Because forensic evaluators must rely on scientifically and professionally derived knowledge when making practiced judgments (American Psychological Association, 2002; Committee on Ethical Guidelines for Forensic Psychologists, 1991, 2005 in preparation) and given the state of our current scientifically based knowledge regarding CSA, psychologists must be conservative in their statements to the general public and the legal system.

When providing information to the legal system, the evaluator should be cautious and make statements that can be supported by scientific data (see Kuehnle, 1998b). The court should be informed of the developmental limitations of memory and interfering factors, such as the alteration of some children's memories through the presentation of inaccurate information. Fisher and Whiting (1998) note the need to limit conclusions in legal proceedings when the questions exceed what one can reasonably answer. These authors provide a variety of examples of how psychological testimony can fail to meet proven reliable methods which have received general acceptance in the scientific community (*Frye v. United States*, 1923), including the misapplication of the diagnosis of post-traumatic stress disorder (PTSD) as an indication of sexual abuse. In the context of CSA allegations, highly publicized convictions have faced reversal by State Supreme Courts based upon the failure of psychological expert testimony to meet evidentiary standards (e.g., *Bussey v. Commonwealth*, 1984; *State of New Jersey v. Margaret Kelly Michaels*, 1993).

When other courts become involved. CSA cases may be litigated across a variety of legal venues, including criminal and civil courts. Civil court proceedings may involve dependency, termination of parental rights, child custody and visitation, and civil proceedings litigated by victims for monetary damages. It is conceivable that a child custody evaluator's case may be litigated in more than one legal venue. For example, when the family court renders a decision that a child has been sexually abused based on the data presented by the custody evaluator, the evaluator may be asked to provide the state attorney with a copy of his/her file for pending criminal proceedings. Although criminal charges may be filed, the evaluator must not release his or her case files to any authority beyond the original court order without a second court order, which directs the custody evaluator to do so.

CONCLUSION

> The child custody court has redefined its mission from deciding *which* parent should receive custody after divorce to determining *how* to involve both parents in the life of a child safely. (Schepard, 2005, p. 4)

Whether a child custody evaluation presents with or without issues of CSA, the evaluator should be thorough and even handed; include appropriate methodology and a parallel evaluation process for each parent; and show an understanding of state statutes, relevant case law, and pertinent research findings. When the special issue of alleged CSA accompanies a litigated child custody evaluation, the motives underlying the allegations should be examined. The use of a multiple hypotheses framework can be developed through delineation of rival hypotheses and the development of a timeline. For example, does the allegation of CSA spring forth from a parent demonstrating appropriate protection or manipulative hostility, a child's attempt to protect a parent, or a child's attempt to protect oneself? The numerous hypotheses and the data that support each possibility should be clearly described in the evaluator's written report. The evaluation should further reflect an understanding of nomothetic data obtained through research and whether or not these data fit the unique idiographic characteristics of the specific child, family system, or parents. The ultimate decision of whether the child experienced an event of sexual abuse is a legal question and, in the opinion of the authors of this article, should not be answered by the forensic evaluator.

Based upon the court's finding on the *ultimate issue*, recommendations should focus on interventions specific to the child's needs and parents' deficits in these complex cases. Custody and visitation determinations will be shaped by findings, such as child abuse, one parent alienating the child from the other parent, the child's estrangement from a parent due to that parent's behavior, and other dynamics. In cases where a parent has been separated from a child due to a false positive accusation of CSA, the evaluator will need to craft a reunification plan specific to the child's age, unique characteristics of the child, and the assets and deficits of each parent. Whether a parent has intentionally used child sexual abuse to manipulate the legal system should weigh heavily on custody considerations. In cases where the child is found to be a victim of incest perpetrated by a parent, the evaluator will need to craft a treatment plan specific to the age of the child, the relationship between the child and incestuous parent, the relationship between the parents, symptoms of trauma, and the relationship between the child and the non-sexually abusive parent.

A brief psycho-educational intervention may be sufficient treatment, when a sexually abused child has few or no symptoms and has a supportive environment. Parent treatment only and parent/child treatment combined are shown to be the most effective in decreasing the child's externalizing behaviors, while child treatment only and parent/child treatment combined are the most effective in decreasing the child's internalizing behaviors. About one-third of sexually abused children will develop sexual behavior problems that should be addressed immediately to prevent harm to other children (Deblinger, Steer, & Lippman, 1999).

Custody cases with allegations of CSA are complex and the novice evaluator may find himself/herself quickly overwhelmed and lost in these tangled webs. It is imperative that the ethical custody evaluator decline these complex evaluations unless he/she has a solid foundation of knowledge and experience in CCCs and CSA from which to operate.

REFERENCES

Achenbach, T. M. (1991). *Manual for the Child Behavior Checklist/4-18 and 1991 profile.* Burlington, VT: University of Vermont, Department of Psychiatry.

Ahrons, C. R. (1994). *The good divorce: Keeping your family together when your marriage comes apart.* New York: Harper Perennial.

Amato, P. R., & Keith, B. (1991a). Parental divorce and the well-being of children: A meta-analysis. *Psychological Bulletin, 110,* 26-46.

Amato, P. R., & Keith, B. (1991b). Parental divorce and adult well-being: A meta-analysis. *Journal of Marriage and Family, 53,* 43-58.

American Psychological Association. (1994). Guidelines for child custody evaluations in divorce proceedings. *American Psychologist, 49*(7), 677-680.

American Psychological Association. (2002). *Ethical principles of psychologists and code of conduct.* Available from, http://www.apa.org/ethics/code2002.html

Austin, W. G. (2000). A forensic model of risk assessment for child custody location law. *Family and Conciliation Courts Review, 38,* 186-201.

Austin, W. G. (2001). Partner violence and risk assessment in child custody evaluations. *Family Court Review, 39,* 483-496.

Austin, W. G., & Kirkpatrick, H. D. (2004). The investigation component in forensic mental health evaluations: Considerations for parenting time assessments. *Journal of Child Custody, 1*(2), 23-46.

Baker-Ward, L., & Ornstein, P. A. (2002). Cognitive underpinnings of children's testimony. In H. L. Westcott, G. M. Davies, & H. C. Bull (Eds.), *Children's testimony: A handbook of psychological research and forensic practice* (pp. 21-35). New York: Wiley.

Baumrind, D. (1989). Rearing competent children. In W. Damon (Ed.), *New direction for child development: Child development, today and tomorrow* (pp. 349-378). San Francisco: Jossey Bass.

Baumrind, D. (1991). Parenting styles and adolescent development. In R. Learner, A. C. Peterson, & J. Brooks-Gunn (Eds.), *The encyclopedia on adolescence* (pp. 746- 758). New York: Garland.

Benedek, E. P., Derdeyn, A. P., Effron, E. J., Guyer, M. J., Hayden, K. S., Jurow, G. L. et al. (1998). *Legal and mental health perspectives on child custody law: A deskbook for judges.* St. Paul, MN: West Group.

Berliner, L. (1998). The use of expert testimony in child sexual abuse cases. In S. J. Ceci & H. Hembrooke (Eds.), *Expert witnesses in child abuse cases* (pp. 11-27). Washington, DC: American Psychological Association.

Bow, J. N., Quinell, F. A., Zaroff, M., & Assemany, A. (2002). Assessment of sexual abuse in child custody cases. *Professional Psychology: Research and Practice, 33,* 566-575.

Briere, J. (1996). *The Trauma Symptom Checklist for Children (TSCC) professional manual.* Odessa, FL: Psychological Assessment Resource, Inc.

Bussey v. Commonwealth, K.Y., 697, S.W. 2d 139 (1984).

Carnes, C. N. (2000). *Forensic evaluation of children when sexual abuse is suspected* (2nd ed.). Huntsville, AL: National Children's Advocacy Center.

Ceci, S. J., & Bruck, M. (1995). *Jeopardy in the courtroom.* New York: American Psychological Association.

Ceci, S. J., & Friedman, R. D. (2000). The suggestibility of children: Scientific research and legal implications. *Cornell Law Review, 86,* 34-108.

Chaffin, M., Lawson, L., Selby, A., & Wherry, J. N. (1997). False negatives in sexual abuse interviews: Preliminary investigation of a relationship to dissociation. *Journal of Child Sexual Abuse, 6,* 15-29.

Children's Defense Fund. (2002). *The state of children in America's Union 15.* Washington, DC: Author.

Committee on Ethical Guidelines for Forensic Psychologists. (1991). Specialty guidelines for forensic psychologists. *Law and Human Behavior, 15*(6), 655-665.

Deblinger, E., Steer, R., & Lippman, J. (1999). Two-year follow-up study of cognitive behavior therapy for sexually abused children suffering post-traumatic stress symptoms. *Child Abuse & Neglect, 23,* 1371-1378.

DeVoe, E. R., & Faller, K. C. (1999). The characteristics of disclosure among children who may have been sexually abused. *Child Maltreatment, 4,* 217-227.

DiPietro, E. K., Runyan, D. K., & Fredrickson, D. D. (1997). Predictors of disclosure during medical evaluation for suspected sexual abuse. *Journal of Child Sexual Abuse, 6,* 133-142.

Drozd, L., & Olesen, N. (2004). Is it abuse, alienation, and/or estrangement? A decision tree. *Journal of Child Custody, 1*(3), 65-106.

Elliott, D. M., & Briere, J. (1994). Forensic sexual abuse evaluations of older children: Disclosures and symptomatology. *Behavioral Sciences and the Law, 12,* 261-277.

Ellis, E. M. (2000). *Divorce wars: Interventions with families in conflict.* Washington, DC: American Psychological Association.

Everill, J., & Waller, G. (1995). Disclosure of sexual abuse and psychological adjustment in female undergraduates. *Child Abuse & Neglect, 19,* 93-100.

Faller, K. (1991). Possible explanations for child sexual abuse allegations in divorce. *American Journal of Orthopsychiatry, 61,* 86-91.

Fergusson, D. M., Lynskey, M. T., & Horwood, J. (1996). Childhood sexual abuse and psychiatric disorders in young adulthood: I. Prevalence of sexual abuse and factors associated with sexual abuse. *Journal of the American Academy of Child Psychiatry, 34,* 1355-1364.

Finkelhor, D., & Jones, L. M. (2004). *Explanations for the decline in child sexual abuse. Juvenile Justice Bulletin-NCJ199-298* (pp. 1-12). Washington, DC: US Government Printing Office.

Fisher, C. B. (1995). American Psychological Association's (1992) ethics code and the validation of sexual abuse in day-care settings. *Psychology, Public Policy, and Law, 1,* 461-478.

Fisher, C. B., & Whiting, K. A. (1998). How valid are child sexual abuse validations? In S. J. Ceci & H. Hembrooke (Eds.), *Expert witnesses in child abuse cases: What can and should be said in court* (pp. 159-184). Washington, DC: American Psychological Association.

Friedrich, B. (2005). Correlates of sexual behavior in young children. *Journal of Child Custody, 2*(3), 41-55.

Friedrich, W. N. (1997). *Child sexual behavior inventory.* Odessa, FL: Psychological Assessment Resources.

Friedrich, W. N., Fisher, J., Broughton, D., Houston, M., & Shafran, C. R. (1998). Normative sexual behavior in children: A contemporary sample. *Pediatrics, 101*. [Online]. Available: www.pediatrics.org/cgi/content/full/101/4/e9.

Frye v. United States, 293 F. 1023 (1923).

Garven, S., Wood, J. M., Malpass, R. S., & Shaw, J. S. (1998). More than suggestion: The effect of interviewing techniques from the McMartin Preschool case. *Journal of Applied Psychology, 83*, 347-356.

Garven, S., Wood, J. M., Malpass, R. S., & Shaw, J. S. (2000). Allegations of wrongdoing: The effects of reinforcement on children's mundane and fantastic claims. *Journal of Applied Psychology, 85*, 38-49.

Ghetti, S., Goodman, G. S., & Eisen, M. L. (2002). Consistency in children's reports of sexual and physical abuse. *Child Abuse & Neglect, 26*, 977-995.

Gonzalez, L. S., Waterman, J., Kelly, R., McCord, J., & Oliveri, K. (1993). Children's patterns of disclosures and recantations of sexual and ritualistic abuse allegations in psychotherapy. *Child Abuse & Neglect, 17*, 281-289.

Goodman, G. S., Taub, E. P., Jones, D. P., England, P., Port, L. K., Rudy, L. et al. (1992). Testifying in criminal court: Emotional effects on child sexual assault victims. *Monographs of the Society for Research in Child Development, 57*(5), 1-142.

Gould, J. (1998). *Conducting scientifically crafted child custody evaluations.* Thousand Oaks, CA: Sage.

Gratz, K. L., & Orsillo, S. M. (2003). Scientific expert testimony in child sexual abuse cases: Legal, ethical, and scientific considerations. *Clinical Psychology: Research and Practice, 10*, 358-363.

Hagen, M. A. (2003). Faith in the model and resistance to research. *Clinical Psychology: Research and Practice, 10*, 344-348.

Hanson, R. F., Resnick, H. S., Saunders, B. E., Kilpatrick, D. G., & Best, C. (1999). Factors related to the reporting of childhood rape. *Child Abuse & Neglect, 23*, 559-569.

Heilbrun, K. (2001). *Principles of forensic mental health assessment.* New York: Kluwer Academic Plenun Publishers.

Henry, J. (1997). System intervention trauma to child sexual abuse victims following disclosure. *Journal of Interpersonal Violence, 12*, 499-512.

Herman, S. (2005). Improving decision making in forensic child sexual abuse evaluations. *Law and Human Behavior, 29*, 87-120.

Johnston, J. R. (1993). Children of divorce who refuse visitation. In C. Depner & J. H. Bray (Eds.), *Non-residential parenting: New vistas in family living* (pp. 109-135), Newbury Park, CA. Sage.

Johnston, J. R. (2005, February). *Children of divorce who reject a parent & refuse visitation: Recent research and social policy implications for the alienated child.* Paper presented at the Association of Family and Conciliation Courts California Chapter Conference, Sonoma, CA.

Johnston, J. R., & Kelly, J. B. (2004). Rejoinder to Gardner's "Commentary on Kelly and Johnston's The alienated child: A reformulation of parental alienation syndrome." *Family Court Review, 42*(4), 622-628.

Johnston, J. R., & Roseby, V. (1997*). In the name of the child: A developmental approach to understanding and helping children of high-conflict and violent families.* New York: Free Press.

Jones, L., & Finkelhor, D. (2001). The decline in child sexual abuse cases. Washington, DC: Office of Juvenile Justice and Delinquency Prevention, US Department of Justice.

Jones, D., & McGraw, E. M. (1987). Reliable and fictitious accounts of sexual abuse to children. *Journal of Interpersonal Violence, 2,* 27-45.

Keary, K., & Fitzpatrick, C. (1994). Children's disclosure of sexual abuse during formal investigation. *Child Abuse & Neglect, 18,* 543-548.

Kellogg, N. D., & Hoffman, T. J. (1995). Unwanted and illegal sexual experiences in childhood and adolescence. *Child Abuse & Neglect, 19,* 1457-1468.

Kellogg, N. D., & Huston, R. L. (1995). Unwanted sexual experiences in adolescents: Patterns of disclosure. *Clinical Pediatrics, 34,* 306-312.

Kelly, J. B., & Johnston, J. R. (2001). The alienated child: A reformulation of parent alienation syndrome. *Family Court Review, 39,* 249-266.

Kendall-Tackett, K. A., Williams, L. M., & Finkelhor, D. (1993). Impact of sexual abuse on children: A review and synthesis of recent empirical studies. *Psychological Bulletin, 113,* 164-180.

Kuehnle, K. (1996). *Assessing allegations of child sexual abuse.* Sarasota, FL: Professional Resource Press.

Kuehnle, K. (1998a). Child sexual abuse evaluations: The scientist-practitioner model. *Behavioral Sciences & the Law, 16,* 5-20.

Kuehnle, K. (1998b). Ethics and the forensic expert: A case study of child custody involving allegations of child sexual abuse. *Ethics and Behavior, 8*(1), 1-18.

Kuehnle, K. (1998c). Child sexual abuse: Treatment issues. In. G. P. Koocher, J. C. Norcross, & S. S. Hill, III (Eds.), *The psychologist's desk reference* (pp. 252-256). Boston, MA: Oxford University Press.

Kuehnle, K. (2002). Child sexual abuse evaluations. In A. M. Goldstein & I. B. Weiner (Eds.), *Comprehensive handbook of psychology, Volume Eleven: Forensic Psychology* (pp. 437-460). New York: Wiley & Sons.

Kuehnle, K., Greenberg, L., & Gottlieb, M. (2004). Incorporating the principles of scientifically based child interviews into family law cases. *Journal of Child Custody, 1*(1), 97-114.

Kuehnle, K., & Sparta, S. (in press). Evaluating child sexual abuse allegations. In S. N. Sparta & G. P. Koocher (Eds.), *Forensic assessment of children and adolescents: Issues and applications.* New York: Oxford University Press.

Lamb, M., Sternberg, K., & Esplin, P. (1994). Factors influencing the reliability and validity of statements made by young victims of sexual maltreatment. *Journal of Applied Developmental Psychology, 15,* 255-280.

Lamb, M., Sternberg, K., & Esplin, P. (1998). Conducting investigative interviews of alleged sexual abuse victims. *Child Abuse & Neglect, 22,* 813-823.

Lamb, M., Sternberg, K., Esplin, P., & Hershkowitz, I., & Orbach, Y. (1999). *The NICHD protocol for investigative interviews of alleged sex abuse victims.* Unpublished manuscript, NICHD, Bethesda, MD.

Lamb, M. E., Sternberg, K. J., & Thompson, R. A. (1997). The effects of divorce and custody arrangements on children's behavior, development, and adjustment. *Family and Conciliation Courts Review, 35,* 393-404.

Lamb, M. E., Orbach, Y., Sternberg, K., Esplin, P. W., & Hershkowitz, I. (2002). The effects of forensic interview practices on the quality of information provided by alleged victims of child abuse. In H. L. Westcott, G. M. Davies, & H. C. Bull (Eds.), *Children's testimony: A handbook of psychological research and forensic practice* (pp. 131-145). New York: Wiley.

Lamb, M. E., Sternberg, K. J., & Esplin, P. W. (2000). Effect of age and length of delay on the amount of information provided by alleged abuse victims in investigative interviews. *Child Development, 71*, 1586-1596.

Lamb, S., & Edgar-Smith, S. (1994). Aspects of disclosure: Mediators of outcome of childhood sexual abuse. *Journal of Interpersonal Violence, 9*, 307-326.

Lawlor, R. J. (1998). The expert witness in child sexual abuse cases: A clinician's view. In S. J. Ceci & H. Hembrooke (Eds.), *Expert witnesses in child sexual abuse cases: What can and should be said in court* (pp. 105-122). Washington, DC: American Psychological Association.

Lawson, L., & Chaffin, M. (1992). False negatives in sexual abuse disclosure interviews. *Journal of Interpersonal Violence, 7*, 532-542.

Leichtman, M. D., & Ceci, S. J. (1995). The effects of stereotypes and suggestions on preschooler's reports. *Developmental Psychology, 31*, 568-578.

London, K., Bruck, M., Ceci, S., & Shuman, D. (2005). Disclosure of child sexual abuse: What does the research tell us about the ways that children tell? *Psychology, Public Policy, and Law, 11*, 194-226.

Lyon, T. D. (2002). Scientific support for expert testimony on child sexual abuse accommodation. In J. R. Conte (Ed.), *Critical issues in child sexual abuse* (pp. 107-138). Newbury Park, CA: Sage.

Maccoby, E. E., & Mnookin, R. H. (1992). *Dividing the child: Social and legal dilemmas of custody*. Cambridge, MA: Harvard University Press.

Martindale, D. A. (in press). Understanding bias and prejudice in custody evaluations. *The Matrimonial Strategist*.

Martindale, D. A. (2005). Confirmatory bias and confirmatory distortion. *Journal of Child Custody: Research, Issues, and Practices, 2*(1/2), 31-48.

McGleughlin, J., Meyer, S., & Baker, J. (1999). Assessing child sexual abuse allegations in divorce custody and visitation disputes. In R. M. Galatzer-Levy & L. Kraus (Eds.), *The scientific basis of child custody decisions* (pp. 357-388). New York: Wiley.

McIntosh, J. A., & Prinz, R. J. (1993). The incidence of alleged sexual abuse in 603 family court cases. *Law & Human Behavior, 17*, 95-101.

Melton, G. B., & Limber, S. (1989). Psychologists' involvement in cases of child maltreatment: Limits of role and expertise. *American Psychologist, 44*, 1225-1233.

Nelson, K. (1993). The psychological and social origins of autobiographical memory. *Psychological Science, 1*, 1-8.

Peterson, C., & Bell, M. (1996). Children's memory for traumatic injury. *Child Development, 67*, 3045-3070.

Peterson, C., & Briggs, M. (1997). Interviewing children about trauma: Problems with "specific" questions. *Journal of Traumatic Stress, 10*, 279-290.

Peterson, C., & Rideout, R. (1998). Memory for medical emergencies experienced by 1- and 2-year-olds. *Developmental Psychology, 34*, 1059-1072.

Pipe, M. E., Salmon, K., & Priestley, G. K. (2002). Enhancing children's accounts: How useful are non-verbal techniques? In H. L. Westcott, G. M. Davies, & H. C. Bull (Eds.), *Children's testimony: A handbook of psychological research and forensic practice* (pp. 131-145). New York: Wiley.

Poole, D. A., & Lamb, M. E. (1998). *Investigative interviews of children: A guide for helping professionals.* Washington, DC: American Psychological Association.

Poole, D. A., & Lindsay, D. S. (1995). Interviewing preschoolers: Effects of nonsuggestive techniques, parental coaching, and leading questions on reports of nonexperienced events. *Journal of Experimental Child Psychology, 60,* 129-154.

Poole, D. A., & Lindsay, D. S. (1997). Misinformation from parents and children's source monitoring: Implications for testimony. In K. P. Roberts (Chair), *Children's source monitoring and eye witness testimony.* Symposium conducted at the meeting of the Society for Research in Child Development, Washington, DC.

Poole, D. A., & Lindsay, D. S. (1998). Assessing the accuracy of young children's reports: Lessons from the investigation of child sexual abuse. *Applied & Preventative Psychology, 7,* 1-26.

Poole, D. A., & Lindsay, D. S. (2002). Children's suggestibility in the forensic context. In M. L. Eisen, J. A. Quas, & G. S. Goodman, (Eds.), *Memory and suggestibility in the forensic interview. Personality and clinical psychology series* (pp. 355-381). Mahwah, NJ: Erlbaum.

Poole, D. A., & White, L. T. (1991). Effects of question repetition on the eyewitness testimony of children and adults. *Developmental Psychology, 27,* 975-986.

Poole, D. A., & White, L. T. (1993). Two years later: Effects of question repetition and retention interval on the eye witness testimony of children and adults. *Developmental Psychology, 29,* 844-853.

Realmuto, G. M., Jensen, J., & Wescoe, S. (1990). Specificity and sensitivity of sexually anatomically correct dolls in substantiating abuse: A pilot study. *Journal of the American Academy of Child Adolescent Psychiatry, 29,* 743-746.

Realmuto, G. M., & Wescoe, S. (1992). Agreement among professional about a child's sexual abuse status: Interviews with sexually anatomically correct dolls as indicators of abuse. *Child Abuse and Neglect, 16,* 719-725.

Reed, L. J. (1996). Findings from research on children's suggestibility and implications for conducting child interviews. *Child Maltreatment, 1,* 105-120.

Roesler, T. A., & Wind, T. W. (1994). Telling the secret: Adult women describe their disclosures of incest. *Journal of Interpersonal Violence, 9,* 327-338.

Sachsenmaier, S. J. (2005). Complex child custody evaluations: Evaluating the alleged incestuous parent. *Journal of Child Custody, 2*(3), 57-97.

Sas, L. D., & Cunningham, A. H. (1995). *Tipping the balance to tell the secret: The public discovery of child sexual abuse.* London, Ontario, Canada: London Family Court Clinic.

Saywitz, K. J., & Moan-Hardie, S. (1994). Reducing the potential for distortion of childhood memories. *Consciousness and Cognition, 3,* 408-425.

Saywitz, K. J., Geiselman, R. E., & Bornstein, G. K. (1992). Effects of cognitive interviewing and practice on children's recall performance. *Journal of Applied Psychology, 77,* 744-756.

Schepard, A. I. (2004). *Children, courts, and custody*. New York: Cambridge University Press.

Smith, D., Letourneau, E. J., Saunders, B. E., Kilpatrick, D. G., Resnick, H. S., & Best, C. L. (2000). Delay in disclosure of childhood rape: Results from a national survey. *Child Abuse & Neglect, 24*, 273-287.

Sorensen, T., & Snow, B. (1991). How children tell: The process of disclosure of child sexual abuse. *Child Welfare, 70*, 3-15.

State of New Jersey v. Margaret Kelly Michaels, 264 N.J. Super 579 (1993).

Sternberg, K. J., Lamb, M. E., Hershkowitz, I., Yudilevitch, L., Orbach, Y., Esplin, P. W. et al. (1997). Effects of introductory style on children's abilities to describe experiences of sexual abuse. *Child Abuse & Neglect, 21*, 1133-1146.

Sternberg, K., Lamb, M., Esplin, P., & Baradaran, L. (1999). Using a scripted protocol to guide investigative interviews: A pilot study. *Applied Developmental Science, 3*, 70-76.

Sternberg, K. J., Lamb, M. E., Esplin, P. W., Orbach, Y., & Hershkowitz, I. (2002). Using a structure interview protocol to improve the quality of investigative interviews. In M. Eisen (Ed.), *Memory and suggestibility in the forensic interview* (pp. 409-436). Mahwah, NJ: Erlbaum.

Summitt, R. C. (1983). The child sexual abuse accommodation syndrome. *Child Abuse & Neglect, 7*, 177-193.

Tang, C. S. (2002). Childhood experience of sexual abuse among Hong Kong Chinese college students. *Child Abuse & Neglect, 26*, 23-37.

Thoennes, N., & Tjaden, P. (1990). The extent, nature, and validity of sexual abuse allegations in custody/visitation disputes. *Child Abuse and Neglect, 14*, 151-163.

U.S. Department of Health & Human Services. (1991, May). *Monthly vital statistics report: Final data from the National Center of Health Statistics*. Washington, DC: Author.

Warren, A. R., Woodall, C. E., Hunt, J. S., & Perry, N. W. (1996). "It sounds good in theory, but . . .": Do investigative interviewers follow guidelines based on memory research? *Child Maltreatment, 1*, 231-245.

Wolfe, D. A., & Legate, B. L. (2003). Expert opinion on child sexual abuse: Separating myths from reality. *Clinical Psychology: Research and Practice, 10*, 339-343.

Wood, J. M., McClure, K. A., & Birch, R. A. (1996). Suggestions for improving interviews in child protection agencies. *Child Maltreatment, 1*, 223-230.

Correlates of Sexual Behavior in Young Children

Bill Friedrich

SUMMARY. Sexual behavior in children ages 2-12 is related to a variety of environmental, child-specific, and reporter-related variables. This paper reviews correlational research that has examined the relationship of sexual behavior to the variables of sexual abuse, domestic violence, physical abuse, family sexuality, age and gender of the child, child behavior problems, and reporter characteristics. Sexual behavior is directly related to environmental variables that cause dysregulated behavior in children. It is also associated with child behavior problems and varies with age and gender. There are a number of reporter-specific variables, including education level, abuse history, and openness to sexuality, that are also related to the level of reported sexual behavior. The article concludes with a reminder that correlation does not mean causation. *[Article copies available for a fee from The Haworth Document Delivery Service: 1-800-HAWORTH. E-mail address: <docdelivery@haworthpress.com> Website: <http://www.HaworthPress.com> © 2005 by The Haworth Press, Inc. All rights reserved.]*

KEYWORDS. Sexual behavior, family relationships, sexual abuse, dysregulation

Bill Friedrich, PhD, is Professor at the Mayo Medical School and a consultant at the Mayo Clinic. He is an active researcher, clinician, and teacher.

Address correspondence to: Bill Friedrich, PhD, Mayo Clinic, Ge 1B, Rochester, MN 55905.

[Haworth co-indexing entry note]: "Correlates of Sexual Behavior in Young Children." Friedrich, Bill. Co-published simultaneously in *Journal of Child Custody* (The Haworth Press, Inc.) Vol. 2, No. 3, 2005, pp. 41-55; and: *Child Custody Litigation: Allegations of Child Sexual Abuse* (ed: Kathryn Kuehnle, and Leslie Drozd) The Haworth Press, Inc., 2005, pp. 41-55. Single or multiple copies of this article are available for a fee from The Haworth Document Delivery Service [1-800-HAWORTH, 9:00 a.m. - 5:00 p.m. (EST). E-mail address: docdelivery@haworthpress.com].

Prior to the "discovery" of sexual abuse in the early 1980s, sexual behavior of children was rarely the topic of clinical or research commentary. Since then, overt sexual behavior by a child is often interpreted as an indicator of sexual abuse. However, research indicates that sexual behavior is not simply a reflection of sexual abuse. In fact, a variety of sexual behaviors are common in children. Sexual behavior also appears to be related to factors other than sexual abuse (Friedrich et al., 2001).

Sexual behavior seems to share many characteristics with aggressive behavior in children. Both are overt behaviors that have their origin primarily in family practices, although they are also affected by environmental variables (e.g., community violence). Aggressive behavior is related to harsh discipline but is also influenced by many other factors, including exposure to aggression by peers and disruptions in caregiving (Patterson, 1982).

This overlap between the factors associated with both sexual behavior and aggressive behavior is actually rather heartening. The overlap suggests that sexual behavior is a rule-governed construct and can be understood in a similar manner to aggressive behavior. Sexual behavior in children does not have to be mysterious or special. In addition, the research on aggressive behavior in children is huge relative to the research on sexual behavior in children. Inferences that arise from the study of aggression can be used to understand sexual behavior.

Two examples of common behaviors that are prone to misinterpretation can illuminate the relationship between aggressive and sexual behavior.

> *Example 1.* A 5-year-old is sitting in front of the family television. In the middle of an exciting show, he slugs his older sister on the arm. Earlier that day, both children were on a daylong visit with their noncustodial father. The custodial parent wonders what prompted her son to be aggressive. She thinks about the visit and whether their father was overly harsh with them.

> *Example 2.* A 5-year-old is sitting in front of the family television. In the middle of an exciting show, he reaches into his underwear and touches his genitals. Earlier that day, he and his older sister were on a daylong visit with their noncustodial father. The custodial parent wonders what happened at the visit and whether the father did something that made her son behave sexually.

Both of these examples are of relatively common behaviors: sibling conflict that involves hitting on the one hand and touching genitals in a preschool boy on the other hand. In fact, 60.4 % of 2-5 year old boys without a history of sexual abuse were observed to "touch their private parts at home" at least once in the previous six months (Friedrich, 1997). Incidence rates of this magnitude are more likely to indicate a benign explanation for genital touching than a pathological interpretation. This is even more the case if there is no temporal relationship between either of these behaviors and visits with the noncustodial parent (Friedrich, 2002).

What if the behaviors are exhibited more frequently immediately after a visit with the noncustodial father mentioned above, and then decrease in frequency over the week? The behavior can still be understood benignly. The father may not be a direct contributor to its origin. For example, if the parent's relationship is tense, children's self-control abilities are often lowered in these situations. Their behavior becomes more variable as a result. Greater variability increases the likelihood of behaviors that reflect a deficit in self-control. These include crying, anxiety, soiling and wetting, aggression, overactivity, and sexual behavior or comments.

Not only are the sample behaviors relatively common and can be understood benignly, the meaning of the behavior is in part a function of the observer, in this case the custodial parent. What causes one parent to attribute responsibility for the behavior to the father and another parent to attribute responsibility for the behavior to the child being tired at the end of a long day? Parental biases and attributions play a large role in what behaviors are noticed and how they are interpreted (Friedrich, 2002). It is the duty of the mental health professional evaluating complex cases to understand all contributors to the origin of behaviors, including traumatic events, generic life circumstances, developmental progression, and parental attribution.

This paper explicates the research on the correlates of sexual behavior in children. The variables studied include stress, trauma, family circumstances, family sexuality, and parental biases. The paper begins with a caution about what correlations truly mean. In addition, the paper concludes with a discussion of base rates, a concept that can help one understand how to understand the presence of a rare behavior. Most of the research cited utilizes the Child Sexual Behavior Inventory (CSBI; Friedrich, 1997). In its current form, it is a 38-item screening questionnaire of a range of sexual behaviors in 2-12-year-old children. The child's parent or caregiver typically completes it and rates the previous six months.

RESEARCH ON SEXUAL BEHAVIOR

Why does a child exhibit a behavior that adults view as sexual? This question is difficult to answer since it is ethically impossible to do research that can truly inform us as to cause. No institutional research body would allow a study that exposed a child to a sexual stimulus and then measured the child's response. Consequently, we are left with correlations, and thus the title of this paper.

A correlation is a relation between two variables. A coefficient of correlation is an index of the direction and magnitude of a relation. Both of these variables will vary from one individual to the next. This variation gives rise to the term, covariance (Kerlinger & Pedhazur, 1973). For example, pornography in the home is directly correlated with sexual behavior (Friedrich, 2002). This means that more sexual behavior is reported in children whose parents report that pornography is present in their household. The two variables covary in a similar manner.

However, it is not possible to say that pornography caused the behavior. While that is one possibility, it may be that pornography is an indicator of a parent who is more interested in and observant of sexual behavior. The presence of pornography may also indicate a parent who is more open about sexuality. In this situation, the pornography alone may have little to no direct impact, particularly for a very young child. The parent's openness about their sexuality may correlate with a child who is more open about their own nudity, and thus be more likely to "show their body parts to another child."

Correlations vary in terms of size. Their significance is in part a function of sample size and sample diversity. Smaller correlations are significant when sample sizes are larger and the size of the correlation is related to the variance or diversity of the sample. The correlations that are reported for sexual behavior in children are typically small to modest (.15 to .40). This suggests that while there is a relationship, it is neither universal nor uniform. The sample sizes that utilize the CSBI and are cited in this paper are typically quite large and range upwards to several thousand children (Friedrich et al., 1992, 2001; Friedrich, Fisher, Broughton, Houston, & Shafran, 1998; Friedrich, Grambsch, Broughton, Kuiper, & Beilke, 1991).

CORRELATES OF SEXUAL BEHAVIOR

Sexual Abuse

According to a comprehensive review of research to that date (Kendall-Tackett, Williams, & Finkelhor, 1993), sexual behavior problems are the most consistent immediate outcome to sexual abuse. This is true for both children and teenagers according to the majority of the studies reviewed.

Since that review, other papers typically state that increased sexual behavior appears to be the most common sequelae of sexual abuse. For example, 499 sexually abused children were studied to determine the relationship of age of abuse to the number of problematic behaviors (McClellan et al., 1996). The authors reported that earlier abuse was associated with the most sexualized behavior.

Young sexually abused children were discriminated from nonabused children by sexual behavior problems in other studies (Cinq-Mar, Wright, Cyr, & McDuff, 2003; Cosentino, Meyer-Bahlburg, Alpert, Weinberg, & Gaines, 1995; Friedrich et al., 2001). Typically, the comparison samples were not the most optimum and were often children whose lives were less troubled than the sexually abused children, so the differences could have been attributable to variables other than the abuse.

However, sexual abuse does not exist in a vacuum, and family factors serve to both predispose the child to abuse as well as potentiate the negative impact. One could argue that a percentage of the variance related to sexual behavior problems is specific to the sexual nature of the abuse but that another unknown percentage is a function of family pathology and individual variables (Friedrich, 2002).

It is quite difficult to tease out the relative influence of sexual abuse from family factors, including other maltreatment. For example, in the Mother-Infant Project, a 27-year longitudinal study at the University of Minnesota, the sexually abused children in their sample were never just sexual abuse victims (Erickson & Egeland, 1987). Even at a very young age, all had experienced at least one and typically two other forms of maltreatment (e.g., physical abuse, emotional abuse, and neglect).

However, data continues to indicate that sexual abuse does have a specific, sexual impact. For example, sexual abuse but not physical abuse was related to younger age at first coitus and younger age at first pregnancy in 1,026 primiparous, African-American women (Fiscella, Kitzman, Cole, Sidora, & Olds, 1998). The same is true for disturbed sexual behavior as measured by children's self-report on the Trauma Symptom Checklist Children (Friedrich, Jaworski, Huxsahl, & Bengston, 1997) and sexual behavior in very young children as reported by parents on the Trauma Symptom Checklist Young Child (Briere et al., 2001).

Sexual abuse is significantly correlated with sexual behavior for every age and gender group studied with the CSBI (Friedrich, 1997; Friedrich et al., 2001). However, the strength of the relationship varies from one age group to the next and is also dependent on the comparison sample. For example, discriminant analysis, a correlational technique, correctly identifies 71.4 to 86.8% of sexually abused children when the comparison sample is nonabused and typically without psychiatric problems and few stressors in their lives (Friedrich, 1997). This percent discrimination drops when psychiatric outpatients are used as a comparison. For example, based on total sexual behavior, roughly half of 6-9 and 10-12 year old male psychiatric outpatients are classified as sexually abused (Friedrich et al., 2001). Most of the error comes from the increased provocative language and sexual interest exhibited by the outpatient boys.

Why sexual abuse is related to sexual behavior both immediately and long term can be explained best by the principles of developmental psychopathology. All pathology is about development and transactions that occur over time and lead to corrected or uncorrected outcomes. For example, sexuality emerges in all children and proceeds along a course where it becomes increasingly more differentiated and integrated into the child's life. The time course for the emergence of teenage and adult sexuality is common to a large number of children for whom there are no other major stressors.

Sexual abuse can also affect the child's view of the word so that nonsexual stimuli lose importance and other stimuli that have a sexual valence increase in importance (Friedrich, Einbender, & McCarty, 1999; Friedrich & Share, 1997). This child is now more likely to notice sexual content on TV or videos, comment on them, and thus activate a coercive parental response, which only reinforces the behavior for a child who already is more impulsive or prone to coercion themselves.

Sexual abuse also occurs in families where sexual abuse in the parents is more probable (Friedrich, 2002). These families are more likely to model poor boundaries or sexualized interaction. This normalizes the sexual behavior that the child is now exhibiting and limit setting by the parent is either nonexistent or ineffectual. Sexual abuse is also about the loss of control, and efforts to regain control may involve sexual acting out and even coercive acting out. Related to control is that sexual abuse causes the child to become confused about sexuality, and mastery over a confusing situation is a common motivation.

Social learning principles suggest that since an important person modeled sexual activity, the child now finds it compelling and has learned to act in this way (Friedrich, 2002). Other sexual behavior is associated with feelings of vulnerability, and this is reflected in the automatic sexual posturing seen in some sexually abused girls. The fact that the abuse was violent will predispose some children to engage in violent sexual behavior. Finally, since the abuse was eroticizing the child continues to pursue sexual arousal (Friedrich, 2002).

Another possible framework takes into consideration the fact that children who have behavior problems fall into two groups, internalizing and externalizing. Down (1993) has suggested that sexual abuse etches more clearly these extremes with regards to sexual behavior (e.g., inhibition and preoccupation), with these two polarities corresponding to internalizing and externalizing, respectively.

Life Stress

Although sexualization appears to be relatively specific to sexual abuse (more so than symptoms such as anxiety), there is increasing evidence that nonsexually abused children can be sexualized. For example, while Kendall-Tackett et al. (1993) found an average base rate for sexual behavior problems to be 28%, another study found that 17% of physically abused children with no evidence for sexual abuse exhibited sexual behavior problems (Deblinger, McLeer, Atkins, Ralphe, & Foa, 1989). In fact, physical abuse and domestic violence are both correlated with sexual behavior as measured by the CSBI (Friedrich et al., 2001).

Life stress as well as such variables as physical abuse and domestic violence are dysregulating to children and reduce their ability to control and inhibit their behavior. Consequently, they are more likely to act out, including acting out sexually. Some sexually behavior is coercive, and both physical abuse and domestic violence are models of coercion.

Any theory must help us understand why it is that at least half of sexually abused children do not exhibit sexualization, at least in the short-term and on parent-ratings. After taking into consideration measurement error (e.g., parent inability to see sexual behavior problems, reliance on overt behavior as a marker rather than internal cognitions about sex, etc.), the theory would have several parts. The first part is that sexualization will vary as a function of abuse severity and age of the child, with older children better able to inhibit their behavior and also escape the detection of parents. A second part takes into consideration those children who are prone to internalizing behavior, and they are likely to account for a large portion of these 50%. A third part of the theory must explain delayed effects, and these include sexual acting out in the teenager, as well as sexual aversion in the adult.

Developmental Age

Early research has established that sexual arousal (e.g., erections in male infants) can occur as young as infancy, and that toddlers will exhibit hugging and kissing of peers (Rutter, 1971). While this latter behavior is presumably related to modelling by parents, it is also likely to reflect a developing sexuality. Children also are quite interested in parental displays of affection, where babies come from, and a high percentage of preschoolers have been reported to "play doctor" (Larsson, Svedin, & Friedrich, 2000).

The most recent research with the CSBI has demonstrated quite clearly that there are a number of overt, relatively reliably measured behaviors that children exhibit at a reasonably high frequency. These have been called developmentally related sexual behaviors because they seem to vary with age of the child (Friedrich, 1997). These developmentally related sexual behaviors have been calculated for three age groups: 2-5, 6-9, and 10-12 (see Table 1 for more detail). The behaviors include touching their mother's or other women's breasts, touching their genitals, and interest in adult nudity in 2-5-year-old boys and girls. Interest in the opposite sex is the only developmentally related behavior for 10-12-year-old boys and girls. Each of these behaviors was reported to have occurred at least once in the previous six months in at least 20% of the children in a large normative sample (Friedrich, 1997).

While research with the CSBI has demonstrated a drop in overt sexual behavior between the ages of 6 and 10 and then a gradual rise between 11 and 12, the reasons behind this drop are likely to be several, and not simply a function of less overt behavior overall. First, young children are more likely to exhibit overt behavior and less likely to inhibit the expression of impulses. Secondly, older children are able to think about sexual issues and not act on them. Thirdly, older children are better able at being secretive from their parents. This is true not only because they are more adept in this regard, but also because their peer interactions are less well monitored than they were in the past. Finally, there may actually be a change in interests for some children in the same way that young children lose interest in GI Joe or Barbie dolls as they get older and then their interest returns in a new form (e.g., football, fashion, etc.).

Gender

Although the developmentally related sexual behaviors outlined in Table 1 are shared for both males and females, there is one exception: touches sex parts in public for 2-5-year-old girls. This suggests that female children learn earlier than boys to inhibit overt sexual behavior. In fact, the majority of sexual behaviors measured by the CSBI, at the age groups of 2-5, 6-9, and 10-12, find that rates are higher in nonabused males than in nonabused females. This is similar to research that illustrates gender differences in externalizing behavior (Friedrich, 2002).

Behavior Problems

Sexual behavior is directly associated with other behavior problems in children. This is true for both behaviors that are labeled as externalizing (e.g., aggression, hyperactivity) and internalizing (e.g., anxiety, social immaturity). The relationship is most direct for preschool children and less so for older children. The drop in the size of the relationship is due in part to the reduced frequency of overt sexual behavior problems in older children (Friedrich et al., 2001).

Sexual behavior as rated by the CSBI is relatively diverse and includes such behaviors as boundary problems, gender role play, intrusive sexual behavior, sexual knowledge/interest, and self stimulating behaviors (Friedrich, 1997). Sexual knowledge/interest is the behavior cluster with the strongest relationship over all age groups with other behavior problems, and even more so with externalizing behavior in the older age groups. Why that is the case deserves some discussion since it can help to elucidate why children who have other behavior problems may also show sexual knowledge/interest at higher rates.

Sexual knowledge/interest as measured by the CSBI is anchored by items measuring the child's interest in watching movies or video with sexual content, using sexual words, and having more knowledge about sex than other same-aged children the parent knows. Aggressive children are more provocative and often less well monitored by their parents. Provocative children are more likely to use swear words that may have a sexual connotation, or refuse parents commands to not watch movies with age-appropriate sexual content. This refusal is part of the coercive dynamic and may not actually be related to any increased interest by the child (Patterson, 1982). The child has learned that if the parent says one thing, he gets attention if he says the opposite. Children who roam alone or with peers are more likely to observe adult activity or get involved with teenagers whose sexual interest is more overt. Both of these additional environmental influences will manifest themselves in the parent reporting more sexual interest or knowledge.

Family Sexuality

This variable has been studied with several indices of family sexuality. One index measures co-sleeping and co-bathing. Another index measures overt adult sexuality in the form of nudity and sexual behavior. When children live in homes where they have opportunities to observe adult sexuality in any format (i.e., live, video, TV), they exhibit more sexual behavior than do children without that opportunity (Friedrich et al., 2001).

It is quite interesting that in children in the normative sample, who did not have other life events or behavior problems, co-sleeping and co-bathing were not related to sexual behavior for children who were less than 8 years old. This suggests that for families, occasional sleeping in the same bed or showering or bathing with a parent is not a provocative behavior. The frequency of co-sleeping and co-bathing practices dropped off markedly by age 6 in a largely Caucasian and Midwestern sample (Friedrich, 2002).

Reporter Characteristics

The parent is the observer of the child's behavior and often the person who raises concern. Despite that fact, characteristics of the reporter that are related to reporting levels have not been well studied. Literature from other areas of child psychopathology do show that parent features (e.g., depression, anger) are correlated with behavioral reports of their child (Friedrich, 2002). It follows that the same is true for sexual behavior.

Four variables have been studied relatively recently with the CSBI. These include education level of the parent, race, parental attitude toward sexuality in children, and parental sexual abuse history. Many of the findings are unpublished and are reported here for the first time. Parents who are less well educated report less sexual behavior on the CSBI than do parents with more education. The reason for this is unclear but less well educated parents may not be as good an observer of their child's behavior. In addition, they may have more experience with social service agencies and learned to distrust them and thus under-report. Low-income Black parents also report less sexual behavior than do Caucasian parents of similar economic status (Thigpen, Pinkston, & Mayefsky, 2003). A similar set of reasons may apply for Black parents as apply for parents who are less well educated.

Parents who believe that sexual behavior in children is not "normal" report less sexual behavior on the CSBI than do parents who believe it is "normal." This is true even for such normative behaviors as the developmentally related behaviors outlined in Table 1. This particular finding corresponds to results from Swedish and Dutch studies that found generally higher rates of normative sexual behavior in children than did U.S. parents (Friedrich, Sandfort, Oostveen, & Cohen-Kettenis, 2000; Larsson et al., 2000). Both of these cultures are thought to be more sex-positive than the U.S. culture. However, that was not the case with Belgian children, whose behavioral frequency corresponded closely to U.S children and who live in a culture that is thought to be more conservative (Schoentjes, Deboutte, & Friedrich, 1999).

Finally, parents with a sexual abuse history display a variable reporting style. A percentage tend to report more than the usual amount of sexual behavior and another percentage reports less than is typical for that age group. This is true for both children with a history of sexual abuse and children without a history of sexual abuse. This phenomenon

TABLE 1. Developmentally Related Sexual Behaviors

Age 2-5	
Male	**Female**
Stands too close	Stands too close
Touches sex parts in public	
Touches mother's breasts	Touches mother's breasts
Touches sex parts at home	Touches sex parts at home
Tries to look at people when they are nude	Tries to look at people when they are nude
Age 6-9	
Touches sex parts at home	Touches sex parts at home
Tries to look at people when they are nude	Tries to look at people when they are nude
Age 10-12	
Interested in the opposite sex	Interested in the opposite sex

corresponds to Down (1993), who reported that sexual abuse victims display either inhibition or preoccupation with sexual behavior.

One example of the result of this variable reporting pattern is with one of the sexual behaviors from the CSBI, "touches sex parts at home." For 2-5-year-old boys, 60.4% of the mothers of non-abused boys reported this behavior but only 58.1% of the mothers of sexually abused boys reported this behavior (Friedrich, 1997). One reason for this difference could be the higher frequency of sexually abused parents in the latter group, with some of those parents falling into the "inhibition" group suggested by Down (1993). This behavior still is discriminatory between the two groups, but primarily based on the average score for this item, which is significantly higher for the sexually abused group.

BASE RATES

The concept of base rates, or the rate of the behavior in the populations of concern, is central to understanding the diagnostic utility of a behavior or group of behaviors. Rare behaviors (e.g., homicide) are very difficult to predict with certainty since they are not common in either the clinical samples being studied or the general population.

For example, let us consider a sexual behavior that is very concerning to parents and caregivers. It is a rare individual who does not wonder about the probability of sexual abuse when they hear of a child who "touches another child's sex parts" (item 9 on the CSBI). For example, parents of 10-12-year-old boys without a history of sexual abuse report this behavior to occur in 1.2% of boys while parents of 10-12-year-old boys with a history of sexual abuse report the behavioral frequency to be 27.3% (Friedrich, 1997). If you do not consider base rates, this differential suggests that sexually abused boys are approximately 23 times (27.3 divided by 1.2) more likely to exhibit this behavior.

If you consider the base rate of sexual abuse in this age group to be 5%, based on lifetime abuse rates for males of 8-10%, then you have a different picture. Let us posit that the child in question lives in a town with 27,000 10-12-year-old boys. A 5% rate of abuse identifies 1,350 of these boys as having a history of sexual abuse, and this leaves 25,650 non-abused 10-12-year-old boys. These frequencies are then multiplied by the incidence of a single behavior, with the numbers taken from the CSBI manual (see Table 2 for more detail).

The 23:1 ratio now drops to a 1.2:1 ratio, and the diagnostic utility of this single behavior for this age group is now significantly reduced. This

TABLE 2. Base Rate Explanation

Base Rate Calculation

(% of sexual behavior problems
in a town of 27,000 children
with or without a history of sexual abuse)

Sexually Abused	Non Sexually Abused
1350	25650
x .273	x .012
368	**308**

Even if sexually abused children are **23** times more likely than non-abused children to be sexually intrusive (Friedrich, 1997), sexually abused children are **1.2** times more likely to be identified as sexually intrusive because of differences in base rate and percentage of the sample that is affected by the problem ("touches another child's sex parts" in 10-12-year-old boys).

is one reason why a single behavior should never be cited as an irrefutable indicator of sexual abuse. The diagnostic utility of multiple behaviors does increase the odds of accurate identification of a child, but as indicated above, there are many confounding factors that also have to be considered.

CONCLUSION

It can no longer be stated that sexual abuse is the only or even primary correlate of sexual behavior in children. While it is significant, even when controlling for a variety of child and family factors, other correlations of similar size do exist. These correlations do not imply causality, but they do make interpretation of the behavior more complex and nuanced.

Sexual behavior reflects a child's lack of inhibition and is a manifestation of dysregulation. Environmental factors that increase dysregulation are thus associated with elevations in sexual behavior. These include life stress in general and such dysregulating events as physical abuse and domestic violence more specifically. Aggressive and anxious behaviors are also more likely in dysregulated children and they are correlated with sexual behavior. Sexual behavior typically reduces in observed frequency over time and boys are more overt in their sexual behavior than girls.

Finally, there are features of the reporter of the behavior that need to be considered. Less well educated parents and parents whose culture is more conservative appear to report fewer sexual behaviors than do parents with the opposite features. Reasons for this could include denial, defensiveness, or less acute observation skills than parents who report more normative sexual behavior.

Finally, simply because sexual abuse is correlated with sexual abuse, there is no basis to think that sexual abuse is the sole cause of sexual behavior in a single child. This is due in large part to the fact that correlations do not imply causality. They simply imply a relation, and this relation may be indirect or a function of another, more powerful correlation that is shared among the variables in question.

REFERENCES

Briere, J., Johnson, K., Bissada, A., Damon, L., Crouch, J., Gil, E. et al. (2001). The Trauma Symptom Checklist for Young Children: Reliability and association with abuse exposure in a multi-site study. *Child Abuse and Neglect, 25*, 1001-1014.

Cinq-Mars, C., Wright, J., Cyr, M., & McDuff, P. (2003). Sexual at-risk behaviors of sexually abused adolescent girls. *Journal of Child Sexual Abuse, 12*(2), 1-18.

Cosentino, C. E., Meyer-Bahlburg, H. F., Alpert, J. L., Weinberg, S. L., & Gaines, R. (1995). Sexual behavior problems and psychopathology symptoms in sexually abused girls. *Journal of the American Academy of Child and Adolescent Psychiatry, 34*, 1033-1042.

Deblinger, E., McLeer, S. V., Atkins, M. S., Ralphe, D., & Foa, E. (1989). Post-traumatic stress in sexually abused, physically abused, and non-abused children. *Child Abuse and Neglect, 13*, 403-408.

Down, W. R. (1993). Developmental considerations for the effects of childhood sexual abuse. *Journal of Interpersonal Violence, 8*, 331-345.

Erickson, M. F., & Egeland, B. (1987). A developmental view of the psychological consequences of maltreatment. *School Psychology Review, 16*, 156-168.

Fiscella, K., Kitzman, H. J., Cole, R. E., Sidora, K. J., & Olds, D. (1998). Does child abuse predict adolescent pregnancy? *Pediatrics, 101*, 620-624.

Friedrich, W. N. (1997). *Child Sexual Behavior Inventory.* Odessa, FL: Psychological Assessment Resources.

Friedrich, W. N. (2002). *Psychological assessment of sexually abused children and their parents.* Beverly Hills, CA: Sage Publications.

Friedrich, W. N., Einbender, A. J., & McCarty, P. (1999). Sexually abused girls and their Rorschach responses. *Psychological Reports, 85*, 355-362.

Friedrich, W. N., Fisher, J., Broughton, D., Houston, M., & Shafran, C. R. (1998). Normative sexual behavior in children: A contemporary sample. *Pediatrics, 101*, e9

Friedrich, W. N., Fisher, J., Dittner, C., Acton, R., Berliner, L., Butler, J. et al. (2001). Child Sexual Behavior Inventory: Normative, psychiatric and sexual abuse comparisons. *Child Maltreatment, 6*, 37-49.

Friedrich, W. N., Grambsch, P., Broughton, D., Kuiper, J., & Beilke, R. L. (1991). Normative sexual behavior in children. *Pediatrics, 88*, 456-466.

Friedrich, W. N., Grambsch, P., Damon, L., Hewitt, S., Koverola, C., Lang, R. et al. (1992). The Child Sexual Behavior Inventory: Normative and clinical contrasts. *Psychological Assessment, 4*, 303-311.

Friedrich, W. N., Jaworski, T. M., Huxsahl, J., & Bengston, B. (1997). Dissociative and sexual behaviors in children and adolescents with sexual abuse and psychiatric histories. *Journal of Interpersonal Violence, 12*, 155-171.

Friedrich, W. N., Sandfort, T., Oostveen, J., & Cohen-Kettenis, P. (2000). Cultural differences in sexual behavior: 2-6 year old Dutch and American children. *Journal of Psychology and Human Sexuality, 12*, 117-129.

Friedrich, W. N., & Share, M. C. (1997). The Roberts Apperception Test for Children: An exploratory study of its use with sexually abused children. *Journal of Child Sexual Abuse, 6*, 83-91.

Kendall-Tackett, K., Williams, L. M., & Finkelhor, D. (1993). Impact of sexual abuse on children: A review and synthesis of recent empirical studies. *Psychological Bulletin, 113*, 164-180.

Kerlinger, F. N., & Pedhazur, E. J. (1973). *Multiple regression in behavioral research.* New York: Holt, Rinehart, and Winston.

Larsson, I., Svedin, C. G., & Friedrich, W. N. (2000). Differences and similarities in sexual behavior among preschoolers in Sweden and USA. *Nordic Journal of Psychology, 54*, 251-257.

McClellan, J., McCurry, C., Ronnei, M., Adams, J., Eisner, A., & Storck, M. (1996). Age of onset of sexual abuse: Relationship to sexually inappropriate behaviors. *Journal of the American Academy of Child and Adolescent Psychiatry, 35*, 1375-83.

Patterson, G. (1982). *Coercive family process.* Eugene, OR: Castalia.

Rutter, M. (1971). Normal psychosexual development. *Journal of Child Psychology and Psychiatry, 11*, 259-283.

Schoentjes, E., Deboutte, D., & Friedrich, W. N. (1999). Child Sexual Behavior Inventory: A Dutch-speaking normative sample. *Pediatrics, 104*, 885-893.

Thigpen, J. W., Pinkston, E. M., & Mayefsky, J. H. (2003). Normative sexual behavior in African-American children: Preliminary findings. In J. Bancroft (Ed.), *Sexual development in childhood* (pp. 241-254). Bloomington, IN: Indiana University Press.

Complex Child Custody Evaluations: Evaluating the Alleged Incestuous Parent

Susan J. Sachsenmaier

SUMMARY. Professionals involved in child custody evaluations are sometimes confronted by the complex issue of one parent accusing the other parent of having sexually assaulted one of the children. There is scant research and theoretical literature to guide the professional in the evaluation of the alleged incestuous parent, or the attorney or judge reviewing such an evaluation. This paper describes the guiding principles of such an evaluation, how to structure the evaluation, methods used for data collection, interpretation of data, and the reasoning processes that lead to an ultimate opinion regarding the allegation. Hypothesis formation and testing is described. The form a recommendation should take given positive assessment findings and negative assessment findings is presented. *[Article copies available for a fee from The Haworth Document Delivery Service: 1-800-HAWORTH. E-mail address: <docdelivery@haworthpress.com> Website: <http://www.HaworthPress.com> © 2005 by The Haworth Press, Inc. All rights reserved.]*

Susan J. Sachsenmaier holds a PhD in Clinical Psychology from the University of Montana. She is a Senior Psychologist with the Department of Health and Family Services in Wisconsin and is also in private practice with Psychology/Law Consultation and Therapy. Her primary area of practice is forensic psychology.

Address correspondence to: Susan Sachsenmaier, PhD, Sand Ridge Secure Treatment Center, Evaluation Unit, 301 Troy Drive, Madison, WI 53704.

Opinions expressed in this article do not necessarily reflect those of the State of Wisconsin Department of Health and Family Services.

[Haworth co-indexing entry note]: "Complex Child Custody Evaluations: Evaluating the Alleged Incestuous Parent." Sachsenmaier, Susan J. Co-published simultaneously in *Journal of Child Custody* (The Haworth Press, Inc.) Vol. 2, No. 3, 2005, pp. 57-97; and: *Child Custody Litigation: Allegations of Child Sexual Abuse* (ed: Kathryn Kuehnle and Leslie Drozd) The Haworth Press, Inc., 2005, pp. 57-97. Single or multiple copies of this article are available for a fee from The Haworth Document Delivery Service [1-800-HAWORTH, 9:00 a.m. - 5:00 p.m. (EST). E-mail address: docdelivery@haworthpress.com].

Available online at http://www.haworthpress.com/web/JCC
© 2005 by The Haworth Press, Inc. All rights reserved.
doi:10.1300/J190v02n03_04

KEYWORDS. Incest, alleged sex offender, evaluation, child custody

STRUCTURE OF THE EVALUATION

Guiding Principles

When evaluating a parent who is alleged to have sexually molested one of his or her children, there are certain principles that guide the structure and interpretation of the evaluation. The first is that there may be primary gain by the parent who is alleging that the other parent is a sex offender. The term "sex offender" raises everyone's level of emotionality and moral concern, and in turn, the decisions that affect the alleged offender's liberty and access to his or her children. Therefore, the evaluator must begin and complete the evaluation with an objective frame of mind, without allowing his or her own emotionality or moral concern to rise and influence the evaluation or its outcome. The second principle is that females rarely sexually abuse children, and when they do, it is generally as a partner to an abusing male. This is not a hard and fast rule, however. There is so little research on female sexual offenders that an evaluator is left without a sound scientific methodology upon which to base the evaluation and conclusion. The third principle is that in the absence of a conviction for or admission of sexual abuse, there is no list of criteria that can prove whether the allegation is true or not. Even an assessment of the validity of a child's statement of sexual abuse does not prove the abuse; it takes a court of law to do that. The third principle is very important, because evaluators will find themselves in the position of hearing lists of accusations against the alleged offender, covering his sexual behavior with his wife or girlfriend(s), use of the Internet or telephone for sexual gratification, his sleeping patterns, and potentially many other areas of his life.

Patterns of Psychological, Lifestyle, and Other Variables

There is no particular pattern of psychological variables, lifestyle variables, or any other variables that can say whether a person is or is not a sex offender. Many research studies support this fact (Harris, Rice, & Quinsey, 1998; Murphy & Peters, 1992). Sex offenders who offend against children are a heterogeneous group with few shared characteristics. They include males and females and vary tremendously in age, personal characteristics, life experiences, economic status, sexual preferences, and history of offending (Salter, 1995). Likewise, "(t)he question of determining whether or not a person has committed a sexual offense is not one that a clinical assessment can address. There are no psychological tests or techniques that indicate whether someone has engaged in sexual behaviors with children . . ." (Becker & Quinsey, 1993, p. 169). This stipulation is broadly based and has been accepted for several years. It is emphasized in the Association for the Treatment of Sexual Abusers (ATSA; 2001) *Practice Standards and Guidelines*:

> 9.03 Members **should** recognize that there is no known psychological or physiological test, profile, evaluation procedure, or combination of such tools that can be used to prove or disprove whether the client has committed a specific (sexual) crime. [Bold emphasis in original, "should" designates a guideline; "shall" designates a requirement.] (p. 8)

The subject must either be adjudicated a sex offender, or pronounce himself to be a sex offender in need of treatment, before he can be labeled a sex offender. Until a person is a known sex offender, clinicians must be careful regarding the risk assessment methods that can validly be applied to him. That is because all of the data on all of the sex offender risk assessment methods that produce actuarial tables or patterns of psychological test scores come from known sex offenders, and therefore cannot be applied to a person who is only an "alleged sex offender." That means an evaluator cannot apply any set of data, whether from a comprehensive evaluation or a risk assessment, to a person who is in a civil proceeding such as a custody suit, with no known sexual offenses in his history, with the determination or implication that those data mean the person is, or is not, a sex offender.

Thus, even if a person shows deviant sexual arousal on a plethysmograph, or deviant sexual interests on an Abel Screen, or shows deception on a polygraph when he denies sexual deviancy, none of these data can be used to say or imply he is a sex offender, or that he committed a sexual crime. A person may show sexual arousal or sexual interest in sexually deviant material, but that does not show that he has acted, or will act, on those characteristics in a way that produces a crime. The reverse is also true. The failure of a person to show deviant sexual arousal on a plethysmograph, or deviant interests on an Abel Screen, may not ethically be used to draw inferences about whether a person did or did not commit a particular offense. Only when a person has a known history of having acted on sexually deviant interests or arousal in a criminal manner can the link be made between interest or arousal and the probability of future sexual crime.

Sequence of Data Collection, Analysis, and the Reasoning Process

The sequence of data collection, analysis, and the reasoning process goes like this: First, researchers identify a group of known sexual offenders; second, they identify the most commonly appearing characteristics in the group of known offenders; third, they gather a large group of normal, non-offending men; and fourth, they use sophisticated statistical analysis to see if the most commonly appearing characteristics in each group can be used to discriminate between the groups. A hypothetical "if–then" equation can be constructed to illustrate this.

> A = known sex offenders
> B = characteristics of sex offenders

We can say, "*if* A *then* B," but notice the emphasis on the *if* variable before the *then* variable. Each probability statement in the hypothetical equation depends on the existence of the "A" factor, the known sex offender. There can be no "if B then A." The outcome variable, B, depends on the foundation variable, A. Probability equations such as this cannot be reversed (unless there is perfect correlation between each variable). We can say, "if this coin is tossed, then it will be heads or tails," but not "if this coin is heads or tails, then it will be tossed."

When a probability equation is reversed, it is an error. Incorrect application of a "reverse probability" is one of the more common errors made when a psychologist is attempting to determine a fact at issue, when that fact remains unknown, such as whether a person committed a sexual offense or whether a child has been sexually molested. Poole and Lamb (1998) make the point that once it is known a child has been sexually abused, then it is more likely that certain symptoms will occur (bed-wetting, nightmares, regression to earlier behaviors, touching genitals, etc.). Nevertheless, the occurrence of those symptoms may be caused by any number of factors, not just sexual abuse. Poole and Lamb provide a lucid example: The probability that 'if a woman is pregnant, then she has had sexual intercourse' is different from 'if a woman has had sexual intercourse, then she is pregnant' (p. 295). In summary then, it is not appropriate to identify characteristics associated with known sex offenders, note that some of them are shown or are not shown by a normal person who is not a known sex offender (even though he may be an alleged offender), and conclude that the person is thereby a sex offender or is not a sex offender.

Once an evaluator of an alleged sexual offender knows what the limits of the science are, it is safe to proceed to what can be done. Therefore, the structure of the evaluation of an alleged sex offender is based on knowing what cannot be done, and only then moves toward what can be done. It is important not to imply at the outset that the evaluator will provide ultimate answers.

COLLECTION OF PERTINENT DOCUMENTS AND INFORMATION

The evaluator begins by obtaining releases of information from the alleged offender whenever possible. The alleged offender should be told that the evaluator is performing as an objective expert who is not invested in proving the alleged offender's guilt or innocence. This should be part of the initial Informed Consent. When an allegation of sexual abuse has been made, it will likely have been reported to the local child protective services, which will have produced documents regarding their investigation of the allegation. If the allegation has not been reported to child protective services and it is not entirely spurious (i.e., if it warrants an evaluation of an alleged perpetrator), then it should be reported and that investigation allowed to proceed prior to evaluating the alleged perpetrator. A finding by child protective services that the abuse cannot be substantiated does not negate the evaluation of the alleged perpetrator, but does provide important findings for the evaluator to review. In some states, child protective services automatically notify the police and the investigation is undertaken conjointly. All documents produced by child protective services and police should be obtained. A copy of the transcript of any interviews undertaken with the alleged victim should be obtained, if possible, along with any affidavits provided by involved parties. If the child has been in treatment for the alleged abuse or for other reasons, it may be helpful to review the treatment notes.

Any records that might support or refute the allegation should be obtained, such as phone bills showing calls to sexual-fantasy services (or lack thereof if an allegation has been made regarding phone calls), Internet chat room dialogues, letters, photographs, and so on. The police can search the alleged offender's computer hard drive to see if child pornography has been downloaded or if child pornography Web sites have been visited. Ask both the accuser and the alleged perpetrator what records she and he think are important for the evaluator to review. Also ask both parties which third parties they believe it would be helpful for the evaluator to interview and why. If either parent has kept a behavioral log or other type of systematic data collection, this may be reviewed. In summary, it is better to review too much data, and weigh the credibility of each source, sorting the useful from the non-useful, rather than ignore data that might be useful.

INSTRUMENTS AND METHODS

Forensic Assessment and Categories of Assessment

When choosing which instruments and tests to use, it is important to remember that a custody evaluation takes place in a forensic context and important decisions regarding people's lives and liberty will be made. Chosen instruments and methods should meet the burden of proof established by the legal profession. It is necessary to distinguish between criminal and civil cases. In criminal cases, the burden of proof is "beyond a reasonable doubt" and expert evidence is more likely to be subject to pretrial admissibility hearings in which the reliability and validity of assessment methods can be attacked. The burden of proof in civil hearings is either "clear and convincing" or "preponderence of the evidence" and expert evidence is much less likely to be subject to pretrial admissibility hearings, but is subject to rebuttal by an expert during the hearing. In some cases, a method might be admissible in a civil context but not a criminal context, and this should be made clear. For example, the Abel assessment has been coming under increasing attack during pretrial admissibility hearings and during civil sexually violent person hearings, but has made it into some custody hearings. Another example is the penile plethysmograph (PPG), which has been excluded at every published pretrial admissibility hearing, but is routinely used for pre-sentencing determinations and post-sentencing in probation or parole revocation hearings, and to determine treatment progress.

There are myriad assessment instruments from which to choose when evaluating an alleged incest offender. Generally, the approach to the evaluation is to structure it as a psycho-sexual evaluation, including components of a psychological assessment and sexual history and current sexual behavior assessment. Formal risk assessment focuses on the risk for reoffense of known sex offenders, so for reasons explained above, this type of assessment is usually inappropriate. In cases where the alleged offender has a history of admitting to or having been convicted of a sexual offense, the situation changes. Assessment methods are chosen in seven categories: (a) psychological functioning, (b) sexual history, (c) self-reported sexual interests, (d) psychophysiological assessment of sexual arousal patterns, (e) psychophysiological assessment of deception, (f) risk of sexual offense recidivism if the alleged offender has a previous conviction for sexual offending, and (g) face-to-face clinical interview.

Assessment of Psychological Functioning

The psychological portion of the evaluation should include tests of general psychological functioning and personality patterns, such as the Minnesota Multiphasic Personality Inventory-2 (MMPI-2) or the Personality Assessment Inventory (PAI). It is better to choose tests that have solid reliability and validity indices, rather than little known or insufficiently supported tests (such as sentence completion tests or other projective tests and lesser known personality inventories) because the gravity of the decisions being made demand the best instrumentation. It is advisable to choose tests that have been normed on a normal population, not just a clinical population (e.g., the MCMI-III), or the person being evaluated may appear more or less disturbed than is really the case.

Minnesota Multiphasic Personality Inventory

The MMPI-2 is a popular objective, self-report, true-false personality inventory whose use dates back to its original publication (MMPI) in 1943. There are several validity scales and 10 clinical scales. The test is hugely popular among clinicians and has been extensively researched. A comprehensive review of the MMPI is beyond the scope of this article and the reader is referred to texts such as those by Graham (2000) and Greene (1991). Efforts to define a sex offender typology using MMPI scales goes back nearly half a century (Swenson & Grimes, 1958), with methodological problems with this sort of study described by researchers (e.g., Reppucci & Clingempeel, 1978). Several studies have shown an inability to develop a taxonomy of sex offenders based on MMPI scores (Hall, Graham, & Shepherd, 1991; Langevin, Wright, & Handy, 1990a; Schlank, 1995; Walters, 1987). Some research has shown promise at using the MMPI to differentiate known sex offenders from normal controls (Langevin, Wright, & Handy, 1990b), but only with complicated statistical procedures. One study found 43 different two-point code types among a sample of 403 convicted sex offenders (Erickson, Luxenberg, Walbek, & Seely, 1987), reinforcing the fact that sex offenders are a heterogeneous group. Erickson et al. (1987) found that a small proportion of rapists tended to score higher on scales 4 and 8 or 9 (psychopathic deviance, schizophrenia, and hypomania, respectively), homosexual offenders on scale 5 (masculinity/femininity), and child molesters on scales 4 and 2 (depression), but these profiles made up no more than 21% of any group and were commonly seen among other groups, as well. Further, 19% of the convicted offenders had profiles within normal limits. Graham (2000) notes that while sexual deviation is common among people who score high on scales 4 and 8, and scale 5 may be high among some sex offenders, there can be no prediction of these problems from individual cases.

Some research has tried to identify the differences between incest and non-incest offenders. One early study (Patton, 1979) compared MMPI profile configurations of incestuous with non-incestuous child molesters, finding that the only difference was that incest offenders scored higher on scale 0, the Social Introversion scale. The profile configurations of both groups showed patterns of self-alienation, despondency, rigidity, inhibition, insecurity, and feelings of inadequacy regarding heterosexual relationships. This study used a small sample size (35 incest offenders and 28 non-incest offenders) and has not been replicated; and of course, many people show these personality characteristics without committing sexual crimes. Another study examined the MMPI profiles of 90 men undergoing evaluation for a treatment program for offenders against children (Shealy, Kalichman, Henderson, Szymanowski, & McKee, 1991), with no attempt to discriminate incestuous from non-incestuous offenders. Of four subgroups identified, two had profiles within normal limits, with one group representing sociopathy and the other emotional disturbance, and the other two groups, both of which had scale elevations, showing either anger and aggression or severe psychopathology. This again demonstrates the wide variability of sex offenders. Another approach has been to see if the MMPI can differentiate among sex offender admitters and deniers (Lanyon, 1993), with the finding that admitters had greater sexual deviance, and non-admitters had no greater defensiveness than admitters.

In addition to the knowledge that an MMPI profile and the scale elevations discussed above cannot identify a sex offender, evaluators must be careful in how they interpret certain other scale elevations that may occur when evaluating an alleged offender. Scale 6 (paranoia) often shows an elevation when the subject has been accused of committing a crime, and may be especially pertinent in allegations of sexual abuse (Caldwell, 1997). Situational factors such as an allegation of being a sexual offender may lead a person to endorse items that deal with feeling that one is being plotted against, talked about, or some other variation of suspiciousness of others. Likewise, elevations on the K scale, which reflect defensiveness, may be common in custody evaluations. Moderate elevation on K may indicate a person who is defensive, or who is presenting himself as adequate, effective, and in control. Scale 5, originally designed to discriminate between homosexual and heterosexual men, was found years ago to be unable to do this, and in fact, may distinguish education and social class better than it reflects a person's identification with masculine and feminine stereotypes. For a male, as the scale score lowers, the more the subject has endorsed items dealing with stereotypical traits of masculinity, such as liking to read mechanics magazines and disliking flower arrangement, and as it rises, the more the subject has endorsed items dealing with a wide variety of interests, including those traditionally associated with females. Although some rapists show low scores on scale 5, indicating what may be an aggressive masculinity, there is no evidence that child molesters show any particular scale score.

Personality Assessment Inventory

The Personality Assessment Inventory (PAI) is a more recently developed self-report personality inventory where the subject indicates gradations of how much each item applies to him or her, rather than being compelled to choose between true or false. The test is much shorter than the MMPI-2, includes current items, and avoids colloquial terms and slang (See Conoley & Impara, 1995, for a full review). There have been few studies to date that deal with sex offenders. In one study (Edens, Hart, Johnson, Johnson, & Olver, 2000), 55 sex offenders were part of a group of incarcerated offenders whose PCL-R (Psychopathy Checklist-Revised) scores were used to see if the Antisocial (ANT) scale of the PAI could predict levels of psychopathy in the offenders. It was found that the PAI had low to moderate diagnostic accuracy in this context. In another study (Caperton, Edens, & Johnson, 2004), the PAI was used to predict institutional adjustment and treatment compliance in a sample of incarcerated sex offenders participating in a mandatory treatment program. As expected, the Antisocial scale of the PAI predicted various forms of institutional infractions, but the Treatment Rejection scale correlated only modestly with treatment non-compliance. Neither of these studies offers useful information when evaluating an alleged sex offender. The clinical profile and interpretive report offered by the PAI may provide important clinical information, however, in the context of the overall evaluation. The PAI offers useful information for both clinical subjects and normal subjects who are not seeking treatment and may not have any psychiatric diagnosis or symptoms beyond expected situational responses such as depression and anxiety.

Millon Clinical Multiaxial Inventory

The Millon Clinical Multiaxial Inventory (MCMI, MCMI-II, MCMI-III) is designed for adults who are in treatment or are seeking treatment. It is an objective, self-report, true-false personality inventory measure whose scales parallel those of DSM-IV personality disorders. There are also clinical syndrome scales for measuring the intensity of acute symptoms of psychiatric distress. Research has focused on the assessment of psychopathology. The test has become popular and is now in its third revision. Numerous reviews and critiques are available (see, e.g., Plake & Impara's *Fourteenth Mental Measurement Yearbook*, 2001). Some research has looked at traits of sex offenders. One of the first studies to look at the MCMI and sex offenders (Chantry & Craig, 1994) looked at recently convicted child molesters ($n = 201$), rapists ($n = 195$), and non-sexually aggressive felons ($n = 205$). Sexual offenders overall were more passive-aggressive, with child molesters showing significantly more dependency, anxiety, and depression than either of the other two groups. Child molesters seemed to form a group with some unique traits that set them apart from other offenders.

Another study (Ahlmeyer, Kleinsasser, Stoner, & Retzlaff, 2003), using the MCMI-III, compared sex offenders to other incarcerated offenders, and then compared child molesters to rapists. The child molesters' scale scores indicated more neurotic, affective, and social impairment than the rapists' scale scores. Statistical analysis showed the Dependent scale to be the most important in differentiating these two types of sex offenders. A study more germane to the purpose of evaluating an alleged child molester compared 24 men who had been diagnosed with pedophilia and were in outpatient treatment to 24 normal controls. The hypothesis was that the Pedophiles would show scale scores on the MCMI-II (and two other, lesser known instruments, the

Temperament and Character Inventory and the Dimensional Assessment of Personality Impairment-Questionnaire) indicative of impulsive aggression (Cohen et al., 2002). Pedophiles showed profound and pervasive psychopathology relative to control participants, but only slight evidence of impulsivity. Rather, the pedophiles' scores on these assessment instruments indicated inhibition, passive-aggression, and harm avoidance.

Application of Psychological Functioning Data
to Alleged Incestuous Parent

Table 1 provides data on the normative group, reliability, and validity of each psychological assessment method discussed above and reviews its appropriateness for assessment of an alleged incestuous parent in child custody proceedings.

Assessment of Sexual History

The sexual history portion of the evaluation is obtained by administering, verbally via interview or via a written questionnaire, a life history of the subject's sexual history and current patterns of sexual behavior. Self-reported current sexual practices, if involving a partner, can be verified by interviewing the partner as part of the collateral third party interviews. Sexual History questionnaires are available from a variety of sources (e.g., Psychosexual Life History Questionnaire, www.nicholsandmolinder.com; and the Clarke Sex History Questionnaire for Males, www.psychassessments.com). A sexual history includes the subject's lifelong exposure to sexual material and sexual experiences, legal and illegal, deviant and non-deviant. Face-to-face interview can clarify ambiguous or unclear responses. The subject may undergo polygraph assessment to determine if he has been honest in his responses to the sexual history items. Table 2 provides information regarding assessment of sexual history methods on the normative group, reliability, validity, and appropriateness for assessment of an alleged incestuous parent in child custody proceedings.

Assessment of Self-Reported Sexual Interests

Self-reported sexual interests may be assessed using the questionnaires described above and more formally by use of a true-false form, a multiple-choice report form, self-report to depictions of human beings

TABLE 1. Assessment of Personality Patterns and Psychological Constructs

Instrument	Normative group	Reliability	Validity	Appropriateness for child custody cases
MMPI-2	Clinical patients, normal controls, incarcerated offenders, known sex offenders.	The MMPI has years of psychometric studies behind it and the MMPI-2 was designed so that much of the original research would also apply to it. Regarding use with sex offenders, elevations on scale 4 replicated across more than one study and more than one kind of offender, but elevation on scale 4 cannot predict sexual offense specifically, nor even criminality in general.	The MMPI's validity has been established for years, but not when used to discriminate between sex offenders and non-offenders. Erickson et al. (1987) found 21% of sex offenders showed an abnormal 2-point code and 19% showed a normal profile; other findings have used small sample sizes and have not been replicated.	Appropriate only to look at general psychopathology, not to attempt to identify who is or is not a sex offender based on any scale combination or special scale. Some code types can be expected with certain types of offenders, but no code type predicts a type of offender or whether someone is an offender. Positive findings on either the clinical or validity scales are not conclusive but do present an area of concern that might be addressed, depending on other data, especially that related to sexual deviance, through treatment or temporary supervision of visitation, until a more clear pattern of the alleged offender's behavior can be established. A response style of dissimulation should be investigated during interview.
PAI	Clinical, normal, and college samples, Whites and Non-Whites.	Test-retest reliabilities (retest interval 3-4 weeks) ranged from .31 to .92 (median .82). The manual author suggests adequate scale and subscale reliabilities. Alpha coefficients of internal consistency for the 22 scales range from .45 to .90 (median .81); from .22 to .89 (median .82); and from .23 to .94 (median .86) for the normative, college, and clinical samples (Conoley & Impara, 1995).	Concurrent validity correlations of the PAI validity, clinical, treatment, and interpersonal scales with several other personality instruments (e.g., MMPI, STAI, Beck Scales, Wahler Physical Symptoms Inventory, Fear Survey Schedule) reveal many small to moderate coefficients, suggesting only relatively modest common variance (Conoley & Impara, 1995).	Appropriate to gain information regarding personality style and functioning and response style. Not appropriate to use to attempt to discriminate an actual sex offender from an alleged offender. Findings of significant psychopathology and defensiveness might indicate a need to refer the subject to treatment and to supervise visitation until a clearer pattern of behavior between the alleged offender and alleged victim can be obtained.

| MCMI-III | Normed entirely on clinical psychiatric subjects in treatment or seeking treatment, 18 years old and up. | No reliability for evaluating alleged sex offenders, unless the subject is in treatment or seeking treatment. | Intended for persons who have psychological symptoms and are being assessed for treatment and evaluation, not valid for others. | Generally inappropriate, as it over-pathologizes normal people. May be useful with subjects who have been previously diagnosed with a psychiatric disorder. |

TABLE 2. Assessment of Sexual History

Instrument	Normative group	Reliability	Validity	Appropriateness for child custody cases
Psychosexual Life History Questionnaire	Not normed	Not tested	Face validity	Appropriate as a self-report history and review of current sexual interests and functioning, not as a determinant of guilt or innocence. Designed for use with persons referred following allegations of sexual abuse. Addresses several broad areas of life history, seeks to elicit subjective feelings and attitudes.
Clarke Sex History Questionnaire for Males	Not normed	Not tested	Face validity	Appropriate as a self-report history and review of current sexual interests and functioning, not as a determinant of guilt or innocence. Twenty-three scales provide a comprehensive sexual history, with focus on various paraphilias, and risk to others.

presented in a visual slide format, or viewing time of human beings presented in a visual slide format.

Multiphasic Sex Inventory

The Multiphasic Sex Inventory (Nichols & Molinder, 1984) is a true-false, self-report form that yields several scale scores encompassing validity (response style), accountability, sexual deviance, paraphilic interests, sexual dysfunction, sex deviance development, marriage development, gender identity and gender orientation development, and sexual assault behavior. Results must be interpreted with great restraint, as this test is used most appropriately as a treatment planning tool with known offenders.

The first MSI was developed using incarcerated sex offenders. Several small studies showed internal consistency, valid item content, and the test's ability to differentiate between treated and untreated sexual offenders. The authors caution that the test should be used only with known offenders, but some scales may provide useful information in an evaluation of an alleged offender, such as scales that report the subject's admission to various paraphilic behaviors, treatment motivation, sexual interests, and sexual knowledge and beliefs. It should be noted that a person might not admit to paraphilic or other deviant behaviors even though he has them, and the test results would then be inaccurate. The MSI sexual history and current sexual interests scales can be compared with the responses provided on the sexual history questionnaire and verified through the polygraph examination. One study administered the MSI to 30 males who were accused of sexual offenses but denied them. All of them eventually admitted to their offenses during treatment. Their MSI scores were compared to those of 140 pre-treatment child molesters. There was a significant difference on the Child Molest Lie Scale (Grier, 1995). This is interesting, but useless because the MSI profile form states that the Lie scale can only be scored if the subject admits his offense.

The MSI-II greatly expanded on the original. The most significant addition is that two new scales, the Molester Comparison and Rapist Comparison Scales, compare the client's scores to the scores of known child molesters and rapists. The manual cautions against using these scores to determine whether someone is or is not a sex offender, a caveat that is strongly emphasized here given the likelihood of an error of reverse probability, as discussed earlier. The MSI-II was extensively validated and cross-validated by the developers, but no studies by independent researchers exist. According to the manual, "Twelve independent replication studies of the MSI II were undertaken using a known-groups method. . . . The cross-validation studies, then, further suggest that the MSI II scales/indices are reliably measuring the behavioral criteria and psychosexual constructs they were intended to measure" (p. 58).

Abel Assessment for Sexual Interest™

Self-report paper and pencil questionnaire. Self-reported sexual interests can also be ascertained using the Abel Assessment for Sexual Interest™ (AASI), which incorporates two measures of self-report interest in sexual stimuli. One measure is a lengthy and detailed questionnaire and the other is the subject's self-report of how arousing or disgusting he believes having sex with the person depicted in the slide would be. The AASI also uses viewing time to assess a subject's interest in certain categories of target victims and paraphilias. Slide categories represent very young girls and boys, young girls and boys, adolescent girls and boys, and adult males and females, with all slides depicting both Caucasian and African-American people. Slides depicting paraphilic interests such as exhibitionism, voyeurism, sadism, and rape are included, but there is no research on the reliability or validity of any categories other than child molesters and rapists. The viewing time measure of the Abel assessment is described as an "objective" measure taken outside of the subject's awareness. This is true of naïve subjects (i.e., those who have not been informed of how the procedure works). Early research on the ability of viewing time measures to identify the subject's area(s) of sexual interest was promising.

Viewing time measurement. The first published study utilizing viewing time by Abel Lawry, Karlstrom, Osborn, and Gillespie (1994) used a set of slides depicting partially clothed and nude people. Research subjects were gathered by choosing men who were referred to Abel and subsequently admitted to sexually molesting a child as the experimental group, and by advertising to pay normal people from the community for their participation as a control group. They measured the length of time each subject looked at each slide. The results of a discriminate analysis and a split-half discriminate analysis (called in the paper "cross-validation") are provided. Results are presented in terms of True Positives (TP, pedophiles accurately identified); and True Negatives (TN, normal men accurately identified). It is not clear what cut off values were used to separate True Positives from False Positives (FP, normal men inaccurately identified as pedophiles), True Negatives from False Negatives (FN, pedophiles inaccurately identified as normal men), or whether there was an "Undetermined" category. In trying to interpret the results provided in the study, if one acts on the basis that any admitted pedophile who was not accurately identified as a True Positive was inaccurately identified as a normal man (False Negative), and any normal man not accurately identified as a True Negative was inaccurately identified as a pedophile (False Positive), the results displayed in Table 3 occur.

In the Male Children's category (on the basis that all subjects were classified), almost one-quarter of admitted pedophiles were inaccurately classified as normal men. The normal men were almost all accurately classified as such. In the Male Teens category, only one-tenth of the admitted pedophiles were misclassified as normal men. In the Female Children's category, most admitted pedophiles were accurately classified, but almost one-tenth were inaccurately classified as normal men. Normal men were more likely to be inaccurately classified as a pedophile when responding to slides of female children, with almost one-quarter mistakenly classified as pedophiles. In the Female Teens category, almost one-quarter of the normal men were inaccurately classified as pedophiles, whereas about five-sixths of admitted pedophiles were accurately classified as such, and the remaining one-sixth were inaccurately classified as normal men. This method of assuming that 100% of subjects were classified is consistent with the way a clinician might report a client's Abel Screen results–as positive or negative for sexual interest in children. The Abel Screen is no longer used, as the Abel Assessment of Sexual Interests has taken its place.

The next study (Abel, Huffman, Warberg, & Holland, 1998) looked at the ability of viewing time, now called Visual Reaction Time (VRT), to classify child molesters accurately according to their target-victim category, and compared VRT to penile plethysmography (PPG). The VRT test is now called the Abel Assessment for Sexual Interests

TABLE 3. True Positives and True Negatives Using the 1994 Abel Assessment

Victim Category	Percent Identified	Victim Category	Percent Identified
Male Children	76% TP + 24% FN (pedophiles) 98% TN + 02% FP (normals)	Male Teens	90% TP + 10% (pedophiles) 98% N + 02% FP (normals)
Female Children	91% TP + 09% FN (pedophiles) 77% TN + 23% FP (normals)	Female Teens	86% TP + 14% FN (pedophiles) 77% TN + 23% FP (normals)

(AASI) to demonstrate its difference from the earlier Abel Screen. Results are provided for True Positives, False Positives, and Percentage correctly classified. There is no "Indeterminate" category. Table 4 displays results showing the percentage of False Positives and percent correctly classified produced by VRT and PPG. The authors concluded that both methods of assessment had high reliability, while the greatest validity was with offenders against male children and male adolescents.

This study was followed up on by Listiak and Johnson (1999) when they compared two methods of PPG with VRT. Preliminary data suggested that the three methods were about equally effective at measuring sexually deviant arousal or interest in eight categories, including F/2-4 (females age 2 to 4), F/8-10, F/14-17, F/adult, M/2-4, M/8-10, M/14-17, and M/adult. However, there were a substantial number of subjects who produced "No response" to any procedure, with the greatest number tending to occur with Male victims of any age, then Female victims age 2-4, then Female victims age 8-10. The highest proportion of significant responses tended to occur to Female victims 14-17 and Female adult victims. Other comparisons were made, but the small number of subjects in each category make meaningful interpretation difficult. This was designed as an ongoing study; unfortunately, funding was cut and the study was terminated (personal communication, Alan Listiak, September 17, 2001).

Probability models. In the largest and most recent study by Abel and his colleagues (Abel, Jordan, Hand, Holland, & Phipps, 2001), the AASI's ability to discriminate child molesters from non-child molesters is analyzed. Incest offenders were systematically excluded because they often offend for reasons other than sexual interest, such as family dynamics and opportunity. Participants included 747 men who underwent AASI assessment as part of evaluation or treatment. The research in-

TABLE 4. Classification of Child Molesters According to Target-Victim Category

Visual Reaction Time	35.2% False Positives for Female Children	65.5% correctly classified
	20.8% False Positives for Female Adolescents	76.7% correctly classified
	04.4% False Positives for Male Children	90.7% correctly classified
	06.5% False Positive for Male Adolescents	91.2% correctly classified
Penile Plethysmography	No variables entered stepwise analysis for Female Children	
	22.7% False Positives for Female Adolescents	71.2% correctly classified
	08.9% False Positives for Male Children	86.8% correctly classified
	06.5% False Positives for Male Adolescents	88.5% correctly classified

volved using half of the subjects to develop a statistical prediction model and the other half to cross-validate it (test it on an independent sample). Men whose income exceeded $60,000 the preceding year or had no income, or who could not read the questionnaire without assistance, were excluded. Groups included admitting child molesters, admitting non-child molesters (e.g., rapists), and "liar-denier" alleged offenders. "Liar-deniers" were labeled such if they were suspected by their therapist of having committed child molestation even though they denied it. Viewing time measures and questionnaire responses were used as potential predictor variables, sorted and weighted by logistic regression.

The predictive model for offenders against girls age 13 and under includes 6 variables: longer VRT to 8-10 year-old females, higher cognitive distortion score, negative response to the question "I feel I am someone children can look up to," self-reported attraction to 8-10 year-old females, self-reported disgust to adult males, and number of times married. At a cut point of .48, this equation correctly identified 74% of true positives (child molesters of girls under 14) and 73% of true negatives (sex offenders who were not child molesters of girls under 14), leaving 26% false positives and 27% false negatives. At a cut point of .88, 25% of child molesters of girls were identified and 99% of non-child molesters of girls were identified, leaving only 1% false positives, but 75% false negatives.

The predictive model for offenders against boys age 13 and under includes 4 variables: longer VRT to 8-10 year-old males, higher cognitive distortion score, being a victim of child abuse more than once, and a higher score on the Hobbies & Interests Scale 1 (visiting the zoo, going to movies or plays, playing team sports, visiting amusement and theme parks, playing video games, science hobbies like astronomy and nature study, collecting things like comic books, arcade games, etc.). At a cut point of .21, this equation correctly identified 86% of true positives and 86% of true negatives, leaving 14% false negatives and 14% false positives. At a cut point of .83, 28% of true positives were identified and 99% of true negatives were identified, leaving 72% false negatives and 1% false positives.

Independent research. Elizabeth Letourneau (2002) received a grant from the Association for the Treatment of Sex Abusers to study the Abel Assessment of Sexual Interest and compare its performance at identifying known sex offenders' preferred target victims to PPG. Subjects were 57 men incarcerated in a high-security military prison for sexual offenses. Subjects completed self-report measures of sexual interest and also underwent VRT, PPG, or both. Both measures did well at identifying molesters of young boys, but neither was able to identify molesters of young girls. VRT did not identify rapists, perhaps because the stimuli were not strong enough, and VRT showed positive responses by nearly all subjects to adolescent females, perhaps because the stimuli were too weak. This study was not considered by the author to be a replication of Abel et al.'s (1998) study because of numerous differences in the stimuli used. Letourneau speculated that the offenders in her sample who had assaulted young girls may have done so for reasons other than sexual interest, echoing the choice made by Abel et al. in 2001, to exclude incest offenders from their study because of their supposed lack of sexual preference for young victims.

Table 5 provides information regarding methods for assessment of self-report sexual interests on the normative group, reliability, validity, and appropriateness for assessment of an alleged incestuous parent in child custody proceedings.

Psychophysiological Assessment of Sexual Arousal

Psychophysiological assessment of sexual arousal is accomplished by penile plethysmography (PPG), also termed phallometry, the measurement of the degree of penile tumescence (sexual arousal resulting in blood flow to the penis) of a subject when exposed to sexual stimuli, visual or audio, including normal and deviant sexual material. Categories of sexual stimuli include different ages, genders, and races, as well as use of force, sadism, and various paraphilias. The premise that makes PPG useful is that someone who sexually offends against a child may have a sexual preference for children and may become sexually aroused to stimuli depicting sexual interaction with children in laboratory assessment. This is not always the case, however, because some sex offenders commit sex crimes against children or adults even when the target victim is not the object of the offender's primary sexual preference. Therefore, PPG results must be interpreted with great restraint. The number of normal, non-offending men who show arousal to deviant stimuli is significant, as is the number of known offenders who do not show arousal to deviant stimuli. Additionally, there are problems with standardization of procedures and associated reliability and validity deficiencies.

PPG has been shown to differentiate between extra-familial (non-incest) child molesters, other sex offenders, and normal non-offenders (Quinsey, Steinman, Bergesen, & Holmes, 1975), but not consistently.

TABLE 5. Assessment of Self-Report Sexual Interests

Instrument	Normative group	Reliability	Validity	Appropriateness for child custody cases
Multiphasic Sex Inventory, 1984	Sexual offenders	Initially, no reliability indices reported, but later research showed that MSI scales demonstrate moderate to high levels of internal consistency (Kalichman et al., 1992) with a sample of incarcerated offenders.	Initial validity shown by item content, three validity scales (social sexual desirability, sex obsessions, and lie scales), and item sorting by judges into paraphilia and other scale categories. Some scales differentiated treated from untreated child molesters in early pilot studies. Later research showed MSI scales demonstrate considerable convergence and divergence with other measures (Kalichman et al., 1992) with a sample of incarcerated offenders. The MSI's most notable limitations are its face validity and potential contamination by response biases.	Self-report questionnaire consists of statements about sexual activities, problems, experiences, sexual deviance and sexual knowledge. May be hand-scored. Most scales are limited to interpretation only with admitted offenders, may provide limited information on some scales for alleged offender evaluation. A deviant profile is more important than a normal profile when evaluating an alleged offender, as many of the items are face valid and could be manipulated by the test taker.
Multiphasic Sex Inventory II	Nationally standardized on 2000 subjects (drawn from a pool of 9000) census matched to 1990 census on age, ethnicity, education, occupation, and marital status, coming from all five geographic regions of the U.S. Spanish translator available. See Nichols & Molinder, 2002.	Coefficient alpha for internal consistency of each scale is provided, ranging from .31 to .94.	Convergent/discriminant, confirmatory factor analysis is provided, along with statement that multiple cross-validation studies provide criterion validity. No independent cross-validation studies are found in the literature (Pubmed and APA electronic databases).	Same as above (MSI) with additional scales and matching of subject to known offenders. Molester and Rapist Comparison Scales compare the client's scores to the scores of known child molesters and rapists. To interpret this would be erroneous (error of reverse probability, see text) and not to be used to determine whether subject is a sex offender; the intention of these scales is to help plan treatment. Must be sent in for scoring. Most useful as a measure of treatment progress with known offenders, but may provide limited information. A deviant profile is more important than a normal profile when evaluating an alleged offender, as many of the items are face valid and could be manipulated by the test taker.

TABLE 5 (continued)

Instrument	Normative group	Reliability	Validity	Appropriateness for child custody cases
Abel Screen, 1994	Self-report questionnaire and slides of partially clothed and nude people, shown to admitted child molesters and community normals	Internal consistency was adequate—subjects who looked longer at one slide representing a slide category tended to look longer at other slides in the same category	High false positives and false negatives in all categories of viewing time measures. Normal men were more likely to be inaccurately classified as a pedophile when responding to slides of female children, with almost one-quarter mistakenly classified as pedophiles.	Unavailable. The 1994 set of stimuli is no longer used.
Abel Assessment of Sexual Interests, 2001 (current version)	Known child molesters, other sex offenders, and alleged offenders who denied child molestation. All incest offenders excluded based on the authors' observation that incest offenders often offend for reasons other than sexual interest.	1998 study on Website provides Cronbach's alpha for each of six slide categories (adult male and female, adolescent male and female, young male and female). When scoring, outliers are removed by statistical process. No test-retest indices. Disclaimer comes with scored test cautioning to use certain values only on the first administration. No known research on reliability of self-report questionnaire.	Internet sites provide information on how to fake the test. Studies show naïve subjects tend to look longer at images that represent their area of sexual interest, e.g., child molesters look longer at slides of children. Attempt by Letourneau (2003) to provide replication of Abel 1998 results failed, were many false negatives using known offenders. Letourneau hypothesized that the child molesters in her sample may have offended for reasons other than sexual interest, that the slide stimuli were not strong enough to interest rapists, resulting in false negatives for that category, and that the female adolescent slide stimuli were too strong and resulted in false positives for that category. Some studies have shown that viewing time has a strong positive correlation with penile plethysmograph results (Abel et al. 1998). The 2001 study reported a wide range of identification of true positives and true negatives, depending on what cut score was used in the algorithm. It is unknown what cut point is used when a subject's results are sent in for scoring.	Many layers of inference make interpretation problematic for decision-making (interest in subject matter is inferred from slide retention time, sexual interest is inferred from subject matter interest, sexual arousal is inferred from sexual interest, past or future sexual behavior is inferred from sexual arousal). Provides probability that person is a child molester of girls or boys or is a liar-denier. To interpret this would be erroneous (error of reverse probability, see text) and not to be used to determine whether subject is a sex offender. Incest offenders systematically excluded from development of probability indices, as were those with incomes greater than $60,000. Must be sent in for scoring. Actual viewing times are not divulged, nor is the scoring algorithm. Also, research has shown a high degree of false negatives and false positives. May be useful as an interview aid or treatment tool. Negative results may not mean that the person has normal sexual interests, but that the person read the Website on how to manipulate test results, or read how the test is scored in *The New York Times* (Bergner, 2005) or in other media.

Scientific experts in the field agree that some men can consciously control their response to the stimuli. For offenders who were able to alter their sexual arousal response in early research studies, data suggested participants were equally successful at suppressing their arousal to preferred stimuli and creating arousal to non-preferred stimuli (see Quinsey & Bergersen, 1976). Important to the current context are findings that incest offenders are the category of sexual offenders who are most likely to show a sexual preference for adults on PPG, but to have sexually molested children (Freund, Watson, & Dickey, 1991). In studies where normal men have been instructed to suppress their sexual arousal to normal sexual stimuli, and to create arousal to male or female children, some have been able to and some have not (e.g., McAnulty & Adams, 1991; Sewell & Salekin, 1997). In a study by Marshall, Barbaree, and Christophe (1986), designed to differentiate among extra-familial child molesters, incest molesters, and non-offenders, the incest molesters were indistinguishable from the non-offenders in response to sexually explicit audiotape stimuli, when all subjects were matched on age, IQ, and socioeconomic status. None of the non-offenders had significant responses to female children age 8 and under, but 14% responded to female teens age 14 and above (Barbaree & Marshall, 1989).

Further complicating the matter is the fact that a significant number of normal men never known to have sexually offended show sexual arousal to deviant stimuli. In one study, 17% of a community sample of non-offenders showed deviant PPG profiles (Farrall, 1991). In research designed by Hall, Hirschman, and Oliver (1995) to study normal men's response to pedophilic stimuli, more than one-quarter of a community sample showed sexual arousal to audiotape pedophilic stimuli that equaled or surpassed their sexual arousal to adult female stimuli, and one-third showed sexual arousal to visual slide pedophilic stimuli that equaled or surpassed their sexual arousal to adult female stimuli. Additionally, some studies have reported a significant percentage of subjects who produce no arousal pattern at all, either normal or deviant, to PPG stimuli (Looman, Abracen, Maillet, & DiFazio, 1998).

Table 6 provides information regarding penile plethysmography on the normative groups, reliability, validity, and appropriateness for assessment of an alleged incestuous parent.

Psychophysiological Assessment of Deception

Psychophysiological assessment of deception, commonly known as the lie detector test, may be useful. "Polygraph" literally means "many

TABLE 6. Assessment of Sexual Arousal

Instrument	Normative group	Reliability	Validity	Appropriateness for child custody cases
Penile plethysmograph	Tested on normals, rapists, child molesters, pedophiles. Definitions of each group have varied among research studies, making it difficult to draw conclusions that are consistent across research studies.	Reliability varies because standardized methodology is not widely used. The Monarch system (Behavioral Technologies, Inc.) in the U.S., and Preftest (Limestone Technologies), in Canada, offer standardized stimuli and interpretation software.	Validity varies with what system is used, increasing when a standardized method is used with autonomic nervous system measures (galvanic skin response, respiration) to detect attempts to suppress arousal. Child molesters who are not pedophiles may not show arousal to PPG child stimuli, rapists may not find the stimuli arousing, offenders may masturbate prior to testing so they show no arousal to any stimuli or may find the stimuli non-arousing, normal men may show arousal to deviant stimuli, and some men can control arousal. Validity is increased when a standardized method is used, with controlled stimuli and interpretive rules. Non-standardized assessment provides no useful information because of unknown erotic stimuli and interpretation rules.	Appropriate, with restrictions. Negative findings are not conclusive, but they do present a lack of evidence upon which to base custody restrictions, in the absence of other reasons to restrict custody or visitation. Positive findings (sexual arousal to children) are not conclusive but do present an area of concern that might be addressed through treatment or temporary supervision of visitation, until a more clear pattern of the alleged offender's behavior with the alleged victim can be established. May be most useful as an interview aid.

writings" and refers to the multiple graphs of physiological function that are taken during the polygraph assessment. Galvanic skin response, heart rate, and respiration are typically monitored. The theory is that these functions of the autonomic nervous system are not within the subject's control and will change when the subject responds to a relevant question with a dishonest answer. There is a pretest interview to be sure the subject understands the questions that will be asked of him, and generally a posttest interview to discuss the findings and clarify the issue when deception has been indicated. The American Polygraph Association (APA) promulgates standards for the examination and for the examiner. Twenty-nine states currently require polygraph examiners to be licensed as proof that they meet the threshold standards set by APA or by the state. There is significant variance in the way polygraph examination results are administered and interpreted. Some examiners use older equipment that may not be as accurate as new equipment. Some examiners read the graphs and provide a subjective decision as to whether deception is indicated. Other examiners use computerized algorithms that provide greater consistency across examiners. A polygraph examination does not include a voice stress analysis (an experimental procedure that lacks scientific acceptance).

The APA (1997) looked at a total of 80 polygraph studies published since 1980 involving 6,380 sets of polygraph examination charts. Researchers conducted twelve studies of the validity of field examinations, yielding an average accuracy of 98%. Researchers conducted eleven studies of the reliability of field examinations, yielding an average accuracy of 92%. Forty-one studies investigated the accuracy of 1,787 laboratory simulations of polygraph examinations, yielding an average accuracy of 80%. Sixteen studies investigated the reliability of independent analyses of 810 sets of charts from laboratory simulations, yielding an average accuracy of 81%. It is unknown why the laboratory simulations were less accurate than the field examinations. There are different ways to decide whether a polygraph is accurate. One way is to count a finding of "Indeterminate" as an error, in which case a review of polygraph accuracy would be much less than if "Indeterminate" findings are removed from the analysis. The APA removes "Indeterminate" findings when calculating accuracy rates.

Many sex offender treatment programs regularly use post-conviction polygraph examination to check on the veracity of the offender's self-reported sexual history. It is important that an offender honestly disclose his full sexual history in order for an effective evaluation of the offender's sexual patterns and offense cycle to be performed and a treatment plan developed. Polygraph assessment often significantly changes what is understood about the offender. For example, Hindman and Peters (2001) reviewed two decades of the first author's research using the polygraph with juvenile and adult sex offenders. They found that when polygraph was used to verify an offender's self report, offenders had underreported their number of assault victims by a factor of 5 to 6, had underreported their juvenile history of sexual assaults, and had overreported their own history of victimization (i.e., offenders lied and said they were offenders because they had been offended against, when they had not been). In order to do this research, offenders were promised immunity from further prosecution.

It used to be that polygraph findings were not admissible during the fact-finding phase of criminal proceedings, so the issue of further prosecution was not a significant deterrent to using the method to detect deception. Gradually, however, polygraph results have been allowed, sometimes using confessions obtained during the pre or posttest interview. In child custody proceedings, where one party is alleged to have sexually assaulted the child, care should be taken to consider the legal issues at stake prior to making the decision to use polygraph assessment. The district attorney should be consulted to find out whether the results would be admissible during criminal proceedings, and if they are, the subject must receive a Miranda type warning before undergoing polygraphy. The APA (1997) provides a list of case citations that deal with the admissibility of polygraph examination results.

The National Academy of Sciences (NAS; 2003) studied the accuracy of the polygraph for the purpose of determining its accuracy as used in employee security screening. They relied mostly on studies that looked at specific-event questioning because that is what virtually all of the research addressed. The NAS noted that although the psychological states associated with deception did rise with deception, they could also rise due to other causes, including anxiety about being tested, being a member of a socially stigmatized group, or being believed by others to be guilty. Additionally, individuals trained in countermeasures could be deceptive but make themselves look non-deceptive, but it was unknown whether polygraph examiners could detect attempts at countermeasures. In spite of these problems, the NAS concluded that specific-incident polygraph testing could discriminate truth telling from lying at a rate much better than chance.

Polygraph errors may result from the examinee not being properly prepared by the examiner prior to assessment, by significant psychophysiological arousal in the examinee not due to deception and not noted by the examiner, by poorly worded questions, or by inaccurate interpretation of the physiological data on the charts. Any error can be damaging, so it is incumbent upon the examiner to follow APA guidelines on proper measures to take both pre and post polygraph assessment. The psychologist should use a reputable polygrapher and consult about issues such as the subject's emotional state, medical history, case facts, and so on.

Cross and Saxe (1992) point out several concerns regarding use of the polygraph in child sexual abuse investigations. They argue that some sex offenders may truly believe that they committed no wrong, and will therefore not show signs of increased autonomic nervous system activity on polygraph assessment, while innocent subjects might show high arousal to relevant questions, not because they are guilty but because they are emotionally aroused by the fact that they are being accused of a crime. No one knows how often false negatives and false positives arise in situations where child sexual abuse is being investigated. Therefore, the authors argue, polygraph assessment should not be used at all.

Faller (1997) reviewed 42 cases in which child sexual abuse allegations were investigated with polygraph assessment, in addition to other investigative procedures. She found that polygraph results were not related to evidence from other sources, including medical evidence, the child's psychological symptoms, the child's statements or demonstrations of sexual abuse, or indicators of sexual abuse from sources other than the child. When alleged offenders passed the polygraph, criminal prosecution was not pursued, but failed polygraphs was not predictive of criminal prosecution. Child protective services' decisions to substantiate abuse was only weakly related to polygraph results, and strongly related to other indicators of sexual abuse. Professional evaluators' decisions about the alleged abuse was most strongly related to the alleged victims' psychological symptoms.

What seems clear from the variability in findings about the validity of using polygraph assessment as a tool in child sexual abuse investigations is that it should be used as only one source of data, in context with many other sources of data. This test should not form the sole basis for a decision about whether an alleged victim was abused.

Table 7 provides information regarding polygraph assessment on normative development, reliability, validity, and appropriate application in child custody cases where one parent is alleged to have sexually abused one of the involved children.

TABLE 7. Assessment of Deception

Instrument	Normative group	Reliability	Validity	Appropriateness for child custody cases
Polygraph	Study participants have varied widely from field studies to laboratory studies, utilizing actual or alleged criminals, employees, or employee applicants, students or normal controls.	Reliability rates reported by the American Polygraph Association range from an average of 81% for laboratory simulations to an average of 92% for field examinations.	According to the American Polygraph Association, a valid examination requires a combination of a properly trained examiner, a polygraph instrument that records as a minimum cardiovascular, respiratory, and electrodermal activity, and the proper administration of an accepted testing procedure and scoring system. Accuracy rates reported by the APA range from an average of 80% for laboratory simulations to an average of 98% for field examinations. The NAS found specific-incident testing accuracy to be well above chance but well below perfection.	May be used as one source of data in the context of gathering multiple sources of data; should not be used as a sole indicator of whether abuse occurred or not.

Assessment of Risk of Recidivism

If a person who is currently alleged to have committed a sexual offense has been convicted of a sexual offense in the past, then one can calculate his risk of sexual reoffense by using unstructured clinical judgment, structured clinical assessment, or an actuarial assessment. Risk evaluators essentially use three types of processes to form their opinion regarding the risk presented by an individual sex offender. The first type of process, and by far the most familiar to courts, is "clinical judgment." In its crudest form, clinical judgment refers to an expert's "gut feeling," whether based on education, experience, or intuition. Clinical judgment may in some cases produce highly valid and applicable results, but in other cases, may produce nothing beyond speculation and personal bias. Whereas clinical judgment has historically received unflattering attention, there are recent studies specific to assessment of dangerousness, including sex offender recidivism risk, that offer a more positive perspective. Thomas Litwack (2001) re-analyzed several studies that compared clinical with actuarial assessment and concluded that clinical judgment should not be abandoned. To overcome some of the disadvantages of unaided clinical judgment, an evaluator may choose structured or guided clinical judgment, which uses a set of empirically based and statistically determined items. The Sexual Violence Risk-20 (SVR-20), developed by Douglas Boer, Stephen Hart, Randall Kropp, and Christopher Webster, was designed as a list of factors to guide clinical judgment. An early study suggested the SVR-20 should be evaluated further before being routinely used to make clinical judgments (Sjöstedt & Långström, 2001), but another study (Dempster, 1998; Dempster & Hart, 2002) reported that the SVR-20 was as accurate as some actuarial measures.

In an actuarial format, each item has been given a weight determined by statistical analysis of how much that item, or variable, contributes to the risk of future dangerousness. The total score falls within a risk category, and is tied to a statistically determined probability that a person who has that score, or falls within that category, will commit a dangerous act. The probability for each category is calculated by identifying a group of convicted sex offenders that fit that category, then determining how long they were in the community following release from confinement before they were reconvicted of (or rearrested for) another sexual offense. Each category then yields the percentage of offenders in that category who were reconvicted at certain specified periods following release. The percentage of recidivism in a category is sometimes referred to as the probability that an offender belonging to that category will be apprehended for another sexual crime if released. This is not technically accurate. A person's score places him in a category composed of a group of research subjects who received scores in the same categorical range. This indicates shared characteristics among the research group members and the individual sex offender. Assumptions about the individual sex offender can be made based on this, but cannot be absolute because the individual offender may have characteristics that are not accounted for by Test X or by the group of subjects who made up the research sample. Table 8 lists characteristics of five actuarial methods: the Static-99, Rapid Risk Assessment for Sex Offender Recidivism (RRASOR), Minnesota Sex Offender Screening Tool-Revised (MnSOST-R), and the Sex Offender Risk Assessment Guide (SORAG); and for one structured clinical method, the SVR-20.

The actuarial methods may often lack utility in evaluations of alleged offenders with no previous sex offender history because the probability of reoffense risk in the lower categories is quite low. For example, for a score of 1 on the Static-99, an offender is placed in a research group that, on follow-up, showed 6% reconviction for a sexual offense at 5 years follow-up, and 7% at 10 and 15 years follow-up. On the RRASOR, a score of 1 indicates 7.6% probability of recidivism at 5 years follow-up and 11.2% at 10 years. Table 8 provides a list of the most commonly used measures of sexual offense recidivism risk and the associated normative groups, reliability and validity data, and the appropriateness for use in child custody proceedings.

Face-to-Face Clinical Interview

The face-to-face interview with the subject should occur after the evaluator has reviewed all records. The subject should be given the opportunity to provide his perspective on the allegations against him and to respond to any issues raised in the records review. The interview is generally semi-structured, going through informed consent, releases of information for collateral sources, a review of the records, current mental status information and self-perception of psychological functioning, administration of assessment instruments, sexual history, and anything else that seems necessary. After the evaluator scores the assessment instruments or receives computerized interpretation, and receives test results from the plethysmographer and polygrapher, it may be warranted to interview the subject again to present conflicting or unexpected results and ask for an explanation.

TABLE 8. Assessment of Sexual Offense Recidivism Risk

Instrument	Normative group	Reliability	Validity	Appropriateness for child custody cases
Static-99	Known offenders upon release from incarceration	Interrater reliability is high when all necessary information is available to score all ten items; .90 reported by both Barbaree et al., 2001; and Sjöstedt & Långström, 2001; and falls when information is missing, e.g., .81 reported by Wong et al., 2000.	Validity is highly supported in U.S. and several countries. ROCs are in .60s-.90s, with lowest at .61 (Firestone et al., 1999) and highest at .93 (Poole et al., 2000, with juvenile offenders); with most falling in the .70s. Developers reported .71 (Hanson & Thornton, 2000).	Inappropriate for an alleged offender. Purpose of Static-99 is to assess recidivism risk in known offenders at their time of release from institutionalization. Revised scoring manual (2003) states method may be applied to alleged offender, but there is no basis for this in the developmental and subsequent literature. If alleged offender is a known offender with a current charge against him for a hands-on sexual offense, the Static-99 can be used.
RRASOR (Rapid Risk Assessment for Recidivism Risk)	Known offenders upon release from incarceration	Interrater reliability is high (.91 reported by Sjöstedt & Långström, 2001; .95 by Barbaree et al., 2001), scoring is on 4 items and follows rules for Static-99 scoring of the same items.	Validity studies are with known offenders. Supportive studies reported in U.S. and 7 countries. ROC of development sample was .71 and cross-validation sample was .67 (Hanson, 1997). Other researchers reported ROCs typically in the 70s, e.g., .73 (Barbaree et al., 2001) and .72 (Sjöstedt & Långström, 2001).	Inappropriate. Purpose is to assess recidivism risk in known offenders. If alleged offender is a known offender with a current charge against him for a hands-on sexual offense, the RRASOR can be used.

TABLE 8 (continued)

Instrument	Normative group	Reliability	Validity	Appropriateness for child custody cases
MnSOST-R (Minnesota Sex Offender Screening Tool-Revised)	Known offenders upon release from incarceration, hands-on offenses only, incest-only offenders excluded.	Interrater reliability reported at .80 in two different studies (Epperson et al., 1999; Barbaree et al., 2001).	ROCs reported by Epperson are .73 (development sample in 1998) to .76 (cross-validation sample in 2000); .65 reported by Barbaree et al. (2001).	Inappropriate. Purpose is to assess sexual violence recidivism risk in known offenders upon release from incarceration, incest offenders excuded.
SORAG (Sex Offender Risk Assessment Guide)	Known offenders, including incest offenders.	Interrater reliability reported by developers in follow-up study is .90 (Rice & Harris, 1999); similar result, .92 reported by Barbaree et al., 2001.	The SORAG is an enhancement of the VRAG (Violence Risk Appraisal Guide, by the same developers). It was hoped it would outperform the VRAG on the prediction of sexually violent reoffense, but it did not significantly do so, for a variety of hypothesized reasons. (It often does as well as the Static-99, RRASOR, or MnSOST-R, however.) ROC of .66 reported by Harris et al., 2003; .63 by Nunes et al., 2002; and .70 by Barbaree et al., 2001.	Inappropriate except for use with previously convicted incest or extra-familial offenders, or those with sex offense charges against them awaiting adjudication.

| SVR-20 (Sexual Violence Risk-20) | SVR-20 is a 20-item checklist of risk factors for sexual violence that were identified by a review of the literature. | No explicit decision-making rules, outcome depends on combination of factors, not just number of factors present. Interrater reliability varies depending on training and amount and type of information available. Some studies done in other countries have not generally been supportive, with the exception of the one noted in the next column. | Focus is on preventing violence in high-risk individuals; items are face valid, no optimization of item selection or weighting based on empirical data. The examiner scores the items and decides on risk level of Low, Moderate, or High, then recommends appropriate interventions. Predictive validity studied on Dutch sex offenders released from psychiatric hospital showed ROC of .80 for sexual recidivism (de Vogel et al., 2004). This sample finding does not generalize to alleged offenders in custody proceedings in the U.S. | May be used if accurate information is available on person being scored, such as on "sexual deviance" variable ("alleged sexual deviance" cannot be scored as "actual sexual deviance") and adequate caution is taken. Primary purpose during development was to assess recidivism risk in known offenders, but can be used with alleged offenders. Three main categories include Psychosocial Adjustment, History of Sexual Offenses, and Future Plans. Low risk indicates no need for interventions, moderate and high risk call for appropriate interventions. There are no studies of this instrument with alleged offenders, so great caution must be exercised in interpretation. |

Development of Hypotheses and Support for Each

The development of hypotheses and determination of how much support each hypothesis receives is the important culmination of the evaluation of the alleged incest offender. The psychologist, as the only mental health professional trained as a scientist (McHugh, 1994; Saari, 1994), holds a great deal of responsibility. There are many decisions to be made throughout the evaluation and in integrating the data at the end. With each decision comes the possibility of error. Clinical judgment must be relied upon as there are no overall actuarial schemes for making decisions that include assessing the credibility of the persons who were interviewed or the credibility of the evidence they purport to be true. All data must be integrated. Borrowing from the model proposed by Kuehnle (1996) in *Assessing Allegations of Child Sexual Abuse*, hypotheses are structured in incremental layers, such as the following:

- The alleged offender probably did not do what he is accused of and he is not at risk to.
- The alleged offender probably did not do what he is accused of but he is at risk to.
- The alleged offender probably did only some of what he his accused of and it does not constitute sexual molestation.
- The alleged offender probably did only some of what he is accused of and it does constitute sexual molestation.
- The alleged offender probably did exactly what he is accused of.
- The alleged offender probably did what he is accused of and more.
- It is not possible to determine whether the alleged offender may or may not have acted in a sexually inappropriate manner, as alleged.

In most cases, there is no way to say with certainty that an allegation of incest is true unless the offender admits his actions in this regard, or the evidence supporting the child's sexual abuse is incontrovertible and other signs point to the parent as the abuser. There is no litmus test, in the absence of medical evidence, for determining whether a child was sexually abused or whether the parent sexually abused the child. The younger the alleged victim is, the truer this becomes. For this reason, it is more accurate and more ethical to report our final opinion as a matter of probability. When a hypothesis cannot be supported to a "probable" level (i.e., more likely than not), the final opinion should state this clearly. Generally, the standard the court will use for the admission of expert testimony is "a reasonable degree of psychological or scientific certainty."

CONCLUSION

The incest offender is the most difficult sexual offender to substantiate because he most often offends, not out of a pervasive deviant sexual interest, but because of opportunity, family dynamics, or some other reason. This paper has provided the research basis for the application of the most commonly used assessment devices when evaluating a parent accused of committing incest.

To summarize the personality assessment literature, there is no typical MMPI/MMPI-2, MCMI (I, II or III), or PAI profile for sex offenders, child abusers or incest offenders, although various forms of pathology do exist in these groups and may show up on personality assessment. On the MMPI, elevations on scale 4 show up on some rapists while elevations on scale 0 show up on some child molesters, but not to the extent that either of these scales can help determine who may be a sex offender. People who harbor attitudes against authority or who have conflicted family lives do not typically act it out by committing a sexual offense, no more than do people who show social introversion. MMPI personality assessment does not help identify the sex offender who is affirming that he is not one. The PAI may offer useful clinical information in the context of the overall assessment, but no specific scale offers information unique to incest offenders or child molesters. The MCMI (I, II, or III) may show elevations on scales that indicate passive-aggression and dependency for child molesters, but none of the subjects studied were separated into groups of incest offenders versus other child molesters.

Summarizing the literature on determining sexual interests, the recent research on the Abel Assessment of Sexual Interest is promising in some aspects, but disappointing in others. Those offenders who were expected to be incest-only offenders were excluded from recent research, as were people whose income in the previous year exceeded $60,000. The probability scores should never be used to help determine whether someone is guilty of a certain crime or might commit a future crime. Additionally, research has shown that most men will show sexual interest in adolescent females, so this category may not be useful in cases where the alleged offender is accused of sexually molesting or propositioning an adolescent female. At its best, the AASI can be a non-intrusive alternative to penile plethysmography. Unfortunately, there are Websites and magazine articles that explain how to manipulate AASI test results.

Studies on the measurement of sexual arousal clearly demonstrate that a person's response to PPG stimuli does not mean they have engaged in or will engage in criminal sexual behavior. Normal, non-offending men may show deviant sexual arousal and never commit a crime; sexual offenders may never show deviant sexual arousal and commit sexual crimes. While PPG results can be useful with known offenders, caution is warranted when interpreting the results of an alleged offender with no history of having committed sexual offenses or shown a history of sexual interest in children or adolescents. While PPG findings are not admissible in the fact-finding phase of criminal justice proceedings, they may still offer potentially useful data in child custody determinations. Using a standardized PPG system such as the Monarch can help provide validity to PPG assessment in the context of alleged incest.

In child custody proceedings where a parent accused of sexually molesting the child is subjected to polygraph examination, a finding of Deception warrants further investigation, but does not provide proof of any sort of past behavior. A finding of Deception should be carefully explored to be sure the examinee understood the questions asked of him and that the questions were properly phrased. A finding of No Deception Indicated does not absolutely absolve the subject from the allegation made against him, but it does provide a lack of foundation upon which to restrict access to the child.

In the evaluation of an alleged offender who is the parent of a child in a custody suit, a normal personality profile, non-deviant sexual history, self-reported sexual interests, and sexual arousal, a non-deceptive polygraph, and lack of a convincing statement by the alleged victim does not mean the person did not commit the sexual offense, but there is a lack of data to support interventions based on the hypothesis that he did. In cases like this, the psychologist has no scientific foundation upon which to recommend that the parent's access to his child be restricted or that the parent must undergo treatment. Abnormal findings along any of these dimensions does not provide proof that the person did commit the sexual offense, but the data may provide the foundation to support certain forms of intervention, such as requiring supervised visitation or that the alleged offender undergo treatment. The child can be protected during supervised visitation while both parent and child can continue to develop a healthy parent-child relationship. Concerns about the parent can be addressed in treatment. During this time, more data can be gathered regarding the relationship of the alleged offender with the alleged victim. As time goes on, if there are signs that the alleged offending parent has improved psychological functioning and a greater understanding of his child's needs of him as a parent, as well as a greater ability to subordinate his own needs to those of the developing child in an appropriate way, short periods of unsupervised visitation may be granted. If all continues to go well with parent and child, these periods of unsupervised visitation may be increased and a more typical shared parenting plan developed.

REFERENCES

Abel, G., Huffman, J., Warberg, B. W., & Holland, C. L. (1998). Visual reaction time and plethysmography as measures of sexual interest in child molesters. *Sexual Abuse: A Journal of Research and Treatment, 10*(2), 81-95.

Abel, G., Lawry, S., Karlstrom, E., Osborn, C., & Gillespie, C. (1994). Screening tests for pedophilia. *Criminal Justice and Behavior, 21*(1), 115-131.

Abel, G. G., Jordan, A., Hand, C., Holland, L., & Phipps, A. (2001). Classification models of child molesters utilizing the Abel Assessment for sexual interest. *Child Abuse & Neglect, 25*, 703-718.

Ahlmeyer, S., Kleinsasser, D., Stoner, J., & Retzlaff, P. (2003). Psychopathology of incarcerated sex offenders. *Journal of Personality Disorders, 17*(4), 306-18.

American Polygraph Association. (1997). *The validity and reliability of polygraph testing.* Available from the American Polygraph Association National Office, 951 Eastgate Loop, Suite 800, Chattanooga, Tennessee 37411-5608. (423) 892-3992 or 1-800-272-8037.

Association for the Treatment of Sexual Abusers. (2001). *ATSA standards and guidelines.* Beaverton, OR: Author.

Barbaree, H. E., & Marshall, W. L. (1989). Erectile responses among heterosexual child molesters, father-daughter incest offenders, and matched non-offenders. Five distinct age preference profiles. *Canadian Journal of Behavioural Science, 21*, 70-82.

Barbaree, H. E., Seto, M. C., Langton, C., & Peacock, E. (2001). Evaluating the predictive accuracy of six risk assessment instruments for adult sex offenders. *Criminal Justice & Behavior, 28*(4), 490-521.

Becker, J., & Quinsey, V. (1993). Assessing suspected child molesters. *Child Abuse & Neglect, 17*, 169-174.

Bergner, D. (2005, January 23). The making of a molester. *New York Times*, retrieved from http://www.nytimes.com/2005/01/23/magazine/23PEDO.html

Boer, D., Hart, S., Kropp, R., & Webster, C. (1997). Manual for the Sexual Violence Risk-20: Professional guidelines for assessing risk of sexual violence. A joint publication of *The British Columbia Institute Against Family Violence* and *The Mental Health, Law, & Policy Institute,* available through Psychological Assessment Resources, Inc., or by calling 604-291-5868.

Caldwell, A. (1997). *Forensic questions and answers on the MMPI/MMPI-2.* Los Angeles: Caldwell Report.

Caperton, J. D., Edens, J. F., & Johnson, J. K. (2004). Predicting sex offender institutional adjustment and treatment compliance using the personality assessment inventory. *Psychological Assessment, 16*(2), 187-191.

Chantry, K., & Craig, R. J. (1994). Psychological screening of sexually violent offenders with the MCMI. *Journal of Clinical Psychology, 50*(3), 430-435.

Cohen, L. J., Gans, S. W., McGeoch, P. G., Poznansky, O., Itskovich, Y., Murphy, S. et al. (2002). Impulsive personality traits in male pedophiles versus healthy controls: Is pedophilia an impulsive-aggressive disorder? *Comprehensive Psychiatry, 43*(2), 127-134.

Conoley, J. C., & Impara, J. C. (1995). *Twelfth mental measurements yearbook.* Lincoln, NE: University of Nebraska Press.

Cross, T. P., & Saxe, L. (1992). A critique of the validity of polygraph testing in child sexual abuse cases. *Journal of Child Sexual Abuse, 1*(14), 19-33.

de Vogel, V., de Ruiter, C., van Beek, D., & Mead, G. (2004). Predictive validity of the SVR-20 and Static-99 in a Dutch sample of treated sex offenders. *Law and Human Behavior, 28*(3), 235-251.

Dempster, R. J. (1998). *Prediction of sexually violent recidivism: A comparison of risk assessment instruments.* Masters thesis, Department of Psychology, Simon Fraser University, Burnaby, Canada.

Dempster, R. J., & Hart, S. D. (2002). The relative utility of fixed and variable risk factors in discriminating sexual recidivists and nonrecidivists. *Sexual Abuse: A Journal of Research and Treatment, 14,* 121-138.

Edens, J. F., Hart, S. D., Johnson, D. W., Johnson, J. K., & Olver, M. E. (2000). Use of the Personality Assessment Inventory to assess psychopathy in offender populations. *Psychological Assessment, 12*(2), 132-139.

Epperson, D. L., Kaul, J. D., Huot, S. J., Hesselton, D., Alexander, W., & Goldman, R. (1999). *Minnesota Sex Offender Screening Tool-Revised (MnSOST-R): Development, performance, and recommended risk level cut scores.* Available at: http://www.psychology.iastate.edu/faculty/epperson/mnsost_download.htm .

Epperson, D. L., Kaul, J. D., & Huot, S. J. (2000, November). *Cross-validation of the Minnesota Sex Offender Screening Tool-Revised (MnSOST-R).* Paper presented at the 19th annual Research and Treatment Conference of the Association for the Treatment of Sexual Abusers, San Diego, CA.

Erickson, W. D., Luxenberg, M. G., Walbek, N. H., & Seely, R. K. (1987). Frequency of two-point code types among sex offenders. *Journal of Consulting and Clinical Psychology, 55*(4), 566-570.

Faller, K. C. (1997). The polygraph, its use in cases of alleged sexual abuse: An exploratory study. *Child Abuse and Neglect, 21*(10), 993-1008.

Farrall, W. R. (1991). *Development of a stimulus set for assessing the arousal patterns of sex offenders using a visual format with audio stories and still photographs.* Unpublished doctoral dissertation, the Institute for Advanced Study of Human Sexuality, San Francisco.

Firestone, P., Bradford, J. M., McCoy, M., Greenberg, D. M., Larose, M. R., & Curry, S. (1999). Prediction of recidivism in incest offenders. *Journal of Interpersonal Violence, 14,* 511-531.

Freund, K., Watson, R., & Dickey, R. (1991). Sex offenses against female children perpetrated by men who are not pedophiles. *The Journal of Sex Research, 28,* 409-423.

Graham, J. R. (2000). *MMPI-2: Assessing personality and psychopathology* (3rd ed.). New York: Oxford University Press.

Greene, R. L. (1991). *The MMPI-2/MMPI: An interpretive manual.* Boston: Allyn and Bacon.

Grier, C. M. (1995, October). Using the Multiphasic Sex Inventory with child molesters. *Psychological Reports, 77*(2), 623-625.

Hall, G. C. N., Graham, J. R., & Shepherd, J. B. (1991). Three methods of developing MMPI taxonomies of sexual offenders. *Journal of Personality Assessment, 56,* 2-13.

Hall, G. C. N., Hirschman, R., & Oliver, L. L. (1995). Sexual arousal and arousability to pedophilic stimuli in a community sample of "normal" men. *Behavior Therapy, 26,* 681-694.

Hanson, R. K. (1997). *The development of a brief actuarial risk scale for sexual offense recidivism.* Department of the Solicitor General of Canada, Ottawa, Ontario. (Available at www.sgc.gc.ca) [Some of these data also described in Hanson, R. K. (1998). What do we know about sex offender risk assessment? *Psychology, Public Policy, and the Law, 4,* 50-72.]

Hanson, R. K., & Thornton, D. (2000). Improving risk assessments for sex offenders: A comparison of three actuarial scales. *Law and Human Behavior, 24*(1), 119-136.

Harris, G. T., Rice, M. E., & Quinsey, V. L. (1998). Appraisal and management of risk in sexual aggressor: Implications for criminal justice policy. *Psychology, Public Policy, and Law, 4*(1/2), 73-115.

Harris, G. T., Rice, M. E., Quinsey, V. L., Lalumière, M., Boer, D., & Lang. C. (2003). A multi-site comparison of actuarial risk instruments for sex offenders. *Psychological Assessment, 15*(3), 413-425.

Hindman, J., & Peters, J. M. (2001). Polygraph testing leads to better understanding adult and juvenile sex offenders. *Federal Probation, 65*(3), 8-15.

Kulichman, S. C., Henderson, M. C., Shealy, L. S., & Dwyer, S. M. (1992, December). Psychometric properties of the Multiphasic Sex Inventory in assessing sex offenders. *Criminal Justice & Behavior, 19*(4), 384-396.

Kuehnle, K. (1996). *Assessing allegations of child sexual abuse.* Sarasota, FL: Professional Resource Press/Professional Resource Exchange, Inc.

Langevin, R., Wright, P., & Handy, L. (1990a). Use of the MMPI and its derived scales with sex offenders I: Reliability and validity studies. *Annals of Sex Research, 3*(3), 245-291.

Langevin, R., Wright, P., & Handy, L. (1990b). Use of the MMPI and its derived scales with sex offenders II: Reliability and criterion validity. *Annals of Sex Research, 3*(4), 453-486.

Lanyon, R. I. (1993). Validity of MMPI sex offender scales with admitters and non-admitters. *Psychological Assessment, 5*(3), 302-306.

Letourneau, E. J. (2002). A comparison of objective measures of sexual arousal and interest: Visual reaction time and penile plethysmography. *Sexual Abuse: A Journal of Research and Treatment, 14*(3), 207-223.

Listiak, A., & Johnson, S. (1999). The measurement of sexual preference: A preliminary comparison of phallometry and the Abel Assessment. In B. K. Schwartz (Ed.), *The sex offender: Theoretical advances, treating special populations and legal developments* (pp. 26-1 to 26-19). Kingston, NJ: Civic Research Institute.

Litwack, T. R. (2001). Actuarial versus clinical assessments of dangerousness. *Psychology, Public Policy, and Law, 7*(2), 409-433.

Looman, J., Abracen, J., Maillet, G., & DiFazio, R. (1998). Phallometric nonresponding in sexual offenders. *Sexual Abuse, 10*, 325-336.

Marshall, W. L., Barbaree, H. E., & Christophe, D. (1986). Sexual offenders against female children: Sexual preferences for age of victims and type of behaviour. *Canadian Journal of Behavioural Science, 18*, 424-439.

McAnulty, R. D., & Adams, H. E. (1991). Voluntary control of penile tumescence: Effects of an incentive and a signal detection task. *Journal of Sex Research, 28*, 557-577.

McHugh, P. R. (1994, December 11). *Educational issues in psychiatry.* Presentation at Memory and Reality: Reconciliation Conference, Johns Hopkins University, Baltimore, MD.

Murphy, W., & Peters, J. (1992). Profiling child sexual abusers: Psychological considerations. *Criminal Justice and Behavior, 19*, 24-37.

National Academy of Sciences. (2003). *The polygraph and lie detection.* Washington, DC: The National Academies Press.

Nichols, H. R., & Molinder, I. (1984). *Multiphasic Sex Inventory manual.* Tacoma, WA: Nichols & Molinder Assessments.

Nichols, H. R., & Molinder, I. (2002). *Multiphasic Sex Inventory II handbook* (3rd ed.). Tacoma, WA: Nichols & Molinder Assessments.

Nunes, K. L., Firestone, P., Bradford, J. M., Greenberg, D. M., & Broom, I. (2002). A comparison of modified versions of the Static-99 and the Sex Offender Risk Appraisal Guide. *Sexual Abuse: A Journal of Research and Treatment, 14*(3), 253-269.

Patton, J. (1979). MMPI profile configurations associated with incestuous and non-incestuous child molesting. *Psychological Reports, 45*, 335-338.

Plake, B. S., & Impara, J. C. (2001). *Fourteenth mental measurements yearbook.* Lincoln, NE: University of Nebraska Press.

Poole, D., Liedecke, D., & Marbibi, M. (2000). *Risk assessment and recidivism in juvenile sexual offenders: A validation study of the Static 99.* Published by Texas Youth Commission.

Poole, D. A., & Lamb, M. E. (1998). *Investigative interviews of children: A guide for helping professionals.* Washington, DC: American Psychological Association.

Quinsey, V. L., & Bergersen, S. G. (1976). Instructional control of penile circumference. *Behavior Therapy, 7*, 489-493.

Quinsey, V. L., Steinman, C. M., Bergesen, S. G., & Holmes, T. F. (1975). Penile circumference, skin conductance and ranking responses of child molesters and "normals" to sexual and nonsexual visual stimuli. *Behavior Therapy, 6*, 213-219.

Reppucci, N. D., & Clingempeel, W. G. (1978). Methodological issues in research with correctional populations. *Journal of Consulting and Clinical Psychology, 46,* 727-746.

Rice, M. E., & Harris, G. T. (1999, May). *A multi-site follow-up study of sex offenders: The predictive accuracy of risk prediction instruments.* Paper presented at the 3rd Annual (University of Toronto) Forensic Psychiatry Program Research Day, Penetanguishene, Ontario.

Saari, C. (1994, December 11). *Educational issues in social work.* Presentation at Memory and Reality; Reconciliation Conference, Johns Hopkins University, Baltimore, MD.

Salter, A. (1995). *Transforming trauma: A guide to understanding and treating adult survivors of child sexual abuse.* Thousand Oaks, CA: Sage.

Schlank, A. (1995). The utility of the MMPI and the MSI for identifying a sexual offender typology. *Sexual Abuse: A Journal of Research and Treatment, 7*(3), 185-194.

Sewell, K. W., & Salekin, R. T. (1997) Understanding and detecting dissimulation in sex offenders. In R. Rodgers (Ed.), *Clinical assessment of malingering and deception* (2nd ed., pp. 328-350). New York: Guilford.

Shealy, L., Kalichman, S. C., Henderson, M. C., Szymanowski, D., & McKee, G. (1991). MMPI profile subtypes of incarcerated sex offenders against children. *Violence & Victims, 6*(3), 201-212.

Sjöstedt, G., & Långström, N. (2001). Actuarial assessment of sex offender recidivism risk: A cross-validation of the RRASOR and Static-99 in Sweden. *Law and Human Behavior, 25*(6), 629-645.

Swenson, W., & Grimes, B. (1958). Characteristics of sex offenders admitted to a Minnesota state hospital for presentence psychiatric investigation. *Psychiatric Quarterly, 32,* 110-123.

Walters, G. D. (1987). Child sex offenders and rapists in a military setting. *International Journal of Offender Therapy and Comparative Criminology, 31,* 261-269.

Wong, K., Flahr, L., Maire, B., Wilde, S., Gu, D., & Wong, S. (2000, June). *Inter-rater reliability of the Violence Risk Scale and the Violence Risk Scale: Sex offender version.* Poster session presented at the annual convention of the Canadian Psychological Association, Ottawa, Ontario.

Rorschach Assessment
in Child Custody Cases

Irving B. Weiner

SUMMARY. This article describes the utility and limitations of the Rorschach Inkblot Test for addressing issues in child custody cases, with particular attention to identifying level of adjustment or psychological disturbance, personality characteristics that may foster or impede adequate parenting, and possible childhood experiences of trauma and sexual abuse. Data are reviewed that document the scientific respectability and widespread use of Rorschach assessment and attest the regularity with which Rorschach-based testimony is admitted into evidence in the courtroom. Also noted are ways in which Rorschach findings can lend incremental validity to forensic evaluations and circumvent efforts at malingering or deception. *[Article copies available for a fee from The Haworth Document Delivery Service: 1-800-HAWORTH. E-mail address: <docdelivery@ haworthpress.com> Website: <http://www.HaworthPress.com> © 2005 by The Haworth Press, Inc. All rights reserved.]*

Irving B. Weiner, PhD, is an ABPP Diplomate in clinical and forensic psychology and Affiliate Professor of Psychiatry and Behavioral Medicine at the University of South Florida. His published books include *Principles of Rorschach Interpretation* (Lawrence Erlbaum Associates, 2003), *Child and Adolescent Psychopathology* (Wiley, 1982), *Psychological Disturbance in Adolescence* (Wiley, 1992), and *Handbook of Forensic Psychology* (Wiley, 1999), co-edited with Allen Hess.

Address correspondence to: Irving B. Weiner, PhD, 13716 Halliford Drive, Tampa, FL 33624 (E-mail: iweiner@hsc.usf.edu).

[Haworth co-indexing entry note]: "Rorschach Assessment in Child Custody Cases." Weiner, Irving B. Co-published simultaneously in *Journal of Child Custody* (The Haworth Press, Inc.) Vol. 2, No. 3, 2005, pp. 99-119; and: *Child Custody Litigation: Allegations of Child Sexual Abuse* (ed: Kathryn Kuehnle, and Leslie Drozd) The Haworth Press, Inc., 2005, pp. 99-119. Single or multiple copies of this article are available for a fee from The Haworth Document Delivery Service [1-800-HAWORTH, 9:00 a.m. - 5:00 p.m. (EST). E-mail address: docdelivery@haworthpress.com].

Available online at http://www.haworthpress.com/web/JCC
© 2005 by The Haworth Press, Inc. All rights reserved.
doi:10.1300/J190v02n03_05

KEYWORDS. Child custody, Rorschach assessment, traumatic stress, sexual abuse, parenting skills

The Rorschach Inkblot Method (RIM) is a personality assessment instrument that provides information about how people tend to make decisions, solve problems, perceive their surroundings, think about events in their lives, deal with their feelings, manage stress, and form impressions of themselves and of other people. Rorschach responses also contain clues to underlying attitudes and concerns that people may not fully recognize in themselves or would be reluctant to report if asked about them directly. Rorschach assessment is appropriate for persons of all ages, except the very young, and normative data are available for adults and for young people at each age from 5 to 16.

The present article first reviews the utility and limitations of Rorschach findings in conducting child custody evaluations, including their relevance to assessing allegations of sexual abuse. The discussion then summarizes research documenting the psychometric soundness of Rorschach findings and their usual admissibility into evidence in forensic cases. Noted in this discussion are reasons to believe that, contrary to concerns raised by some critics of Rorschach assessment, the RIM does not overpathologize, is largely resistant to malingering and deception, and can lend valuable incremental validity to clinical and forensic inferences.

APPLYING RORSCHACH FINDINGS IN CUSTODY CASES

An extensive literature provides guidelines for drawing on Rorschach findings to help identify a broad range of cognitive, affective, and behavioral characteristics (see Exner, 2003; Exner & Weiner, 1995; Weiner, 2003a). Many of these characteristics have a direct bearing on issues of concern to the court in custody cases, particularly with respect to (a) general level of adjustment or psychological disturbance, (b) specific personality characteristics, (c) the possible experience of trauma, and (d) the likelihood of sexual abuse.

Evaluating General Level of Adjustment or Psychological Disturbance

In making determinations of child custody, courts are typically concerned with whether parents and their children are functioning well psychologically or are instead showing signs of adjustment difficulty or disturbance. Having and receiving treatment for a psychological disturbance does not necessarily preclude a person's functioning adequately as a parent. However, severe depression (which could deprive a person of sufficient energy to carry on with everyday responsibilities) and active psychosis (which could prevent a person from being able to distinguish between reality and fantasy) exemplify conditions with a high likelihood of interfering with proper child care.

As for the children in a custody case, indications of serious psychopathology often speak less favorably for the environment in which they have been living than their being free of any major adjustment difficulties. To be sure, psychological disturbance in children cannot be attributed necessarily or solely to their having received poor parental care. Nevertheless, the court is more likely to consider a disturbed child than a well-adjusted child as being in need of a change in environment. Hence, assessments of adjustment level in children, like evaluations of the mental health of their parents, typically assist the court in its custody determinations. Poor adjustment in children may also help to indicate the need for particular kinds of parental attention beyond what young people may ordinarily require.

The RIM provides some well-validated indices that, in concert with information derived from other test data and from observed behavior, help to identify serious psychological disturbance and adjustment problems. These indices include an elevated Perceptual Thinking Index (PTI), which typically reflects disordered thinking and poor reality testing; an elevated Depression Index (DEPI), which is likely to identify some combination of dysphoric mood, negative self-attitudes, and depleted energy; and an elevated Coping Deficit Index (CDI), which usually points to limited coping skills and particular difficulties in establishing comfortable relationships with other people.

To be useful, however, these Rorschach indices should be applied with recognition that each of them tends to generate false negative findings, which means that low scores on them do not warrant ruling out any condition. On the other hand, the PTI and DEPI indices seldom generate false positives, which means that an elevated score on them constitutes strong evidence of psychological disorder. As an example in this regard, Exner (2003, chap. 18) reports research comparing PTI levels among large samples of nonpatients ($n = 115$) and schizophrenia ($n = 170$), affective disorder ($n = 170$), and personality disorder ($n = 155$) patients. Only 3 of the 437 nonschizophrenic respondents in this research showed PTI > 3 (a miniscule incidence of false positive findings), but

44% of the schizophrenia patients had a PTI < 4 (a notable rate of false negatives). Lowering the cutting score to PTI > 2 decreased the false negative rate among the schizophrenia patients to 26%, but also generated a 22% rate of false positives among the nonschizophrenic respondents, primarily in the affective disorder group (see also Ganellen, 1996).

With respect to the CDI, Exner (2003, chap. 16) examined the records of 204 outpatients who complained of difficulties coping with interpersonal relationships and 224 outpatients who did not present any such complaints. Fifty-two percent of those with coping complaints had a CDI < 4, which is a substantial rate of false negatives, but only 12% of the non-complainers showed a false positive CDI > 3.

Some critics of the Rorschach method have alleged that the instrument tends to overpathologize, that is, to suggest psychological disorder when none is present (Wood, Nezworski, Garb, & Lilienfeld, 2001). As noted by Meyer (2001) and Weiner (2001), however, this allegation is based on data drawn from studies involving small and unrepresentative samples of participants who were tested in many instances by inexperienced examiners and sometimes under unusual conditions (e.g., taking the RIM while being told not to move, instructed not to touch the cards, or required to wear electrodes on their head). Inaccurate and misleading allegations of overpathologizing have regrettably made some psychologists leery of using the RIM and some parents wary of taking it during a child custody evaluation. In point of fact, however, the best available normative data make it abundantly clear that elevations in PTI, DEPI, and CDI rarely occur in well-adjusted respondents.

In a normative reference sample of 600 well-functioning nonpatient adults collected in by Exner (2003, chap. 12) in developing the Rorschach Comprehensive System (CS), not one respondent showed an elevation in PTI, just 5% had an elevated DEPI, and the CDI was elevated in only 4%. In a new normative study currently underway for the CS (which is a standardized procedure for administering and scoring the instrument and by far the most widely used system in the United States and worldwide), the first 350 nonpatient adults examined showed similarly low frequencies of elevations on these indices: just one respondent with PTI > 3 (< 1%), 38 with DEPI > 4 (11%), and 25 with CDI > 3 (7%) (Exner, 2002).

As for children and adolescents, the CS normative data include 1,390 young people ages 5 to 16. Not one of these youthful nonpatient respondents showed a PTI > 3, only two of them had a DEPI > 4, and just 168 (12%) received a CDI > 3 (Exner, 2003, Table A.12). Among children, adolescents, and adults alike, then, these three Rorschach indices of serious psychological disturbance or adjustment problems rarely occur in the test records of well-functioning individuals. Their presence in a properly administered Rorschach protocol is therefore unlikely to constitute overpathologizing, but instead gives probable evidence of some psychological dysfunction that merits careful consideration in the course of a child custody evaluation.

Evaluating Specific Personality Characteristics

No single psychological profile identifies the essence of being a good parent, and persons of many different kinds are capable of rearing children in a loving, supportive, protective, and responsible manner. Nevertheless, mental health professionals, specialists in child development and family relationships, and family court jurists generally agree that certain personality characteristics are likely to influence parenting for better or worse. Along with freedom from incapacitating psychological disorder, personality characteristics that usually foster good parenting include (but are not limited to) the abilities to exercise good judgment, make decisions carefully, deal flexibly with problems, maintain reasonably good self-control, and manage stressful situations without becoming unduly upset by them. Also likely to promote positive parenting is being a nurturant and empathic individual who is interested in people, comfortable in close relationships, and able to express feelings and recognize and respond to the feelings of others.

By contrast, a person who is prone to poor judgment, hasty and careless decision-making, an inflexible approach to problem-solving, and impulsive behavior, and who tends to become distraught in the face of even mildly stressful situations, is likely to have difficulty functioning effectively and responsibly as a parent. Similarly, someone who is generally disinterested in people, uncomfortable in close relationships, self-centered and insensitive to the needs and concerns of others, and emotionally detached or withdrawn is at risk for failing to provide the kinds of warmth, nurturance, understanding, and guidance that promote positive personality development in young people.

As readers familiar with Rorschach assessment will recognize, and as elaborated elsewhere (Weiner, 2003a, 2004), each of these personality characteristics is measured by certain Rorschach variables. As a partial list of these variables, the adequacy with which people exercise judgment, make decisions, solve problems, exert self-control, and manage stress can often be inferred in part from the *XA%, WDA%, P, Zd, a:p*, and *D-* and *AdjD-* scores in their record. Level of interest in people, comfort in close relationships, concern about and sensitivity to the needs of others, and capacity to experience and express feelings are often reflected in the *H:Hd + (H) + (Hd), HVI, T, M-,* COP, Fr_+ rF, Egocentricity, *SumC,* and *Afr* scores.

None of these Rorschach variables provides a sole basis for identifying the extent to which any of these personality characteristics is present. Interpreted in an integrated fashion by knowledgeable examiners and weighed in light of the overall configuration of Rorschach findings, however, these variables can shed light on a variety of parental assets and limitations relevant to the issues in custody cases. For all of these variables, moreover, the score levels customarily taken to signify probable functioning limitations occur with very low frequencies in the CS normative sample of well-adjusted adults (Exner, 2003, Tables 12.2 & 12.3).

With respect to specific personality characteristics of children in custody cases, two other Rorschach variables sometimes prove helpful in assessing whether a living situation has been meeting a young person's developmental needs adequately. Among children age 7 or older giving an unguarded record, first of all, an *EA* < 6 is likely to indicate a maladaptive deficiency in coping capacities. Sometimes seen as identifying a developmental arrest, low *EA* in this context usually reflects limited ability to deal with situations by thinking about what they might mean, recognizing and expressing how one feels about them, or deciding what actions they call for. Second, in an unguarded record given by a person age 7 or older, a finding of *T* = 0, especially when *SumShd* > 0 (i.e., there is at least one *C', Y,* or *V* in the record) often indicates limited capacity to form close attachments to other people. A *T*-less record in this context does not necessarily imply avoidance of people, but it does suggest difficulties in anticipating and establishing physically or psychologically intimate relationship with others.

There is no hard evidence concerning the origins of low *EA* or *T* = 0 in a Rorschach protocol. However, these Rorschach findings become relevant in custody evaluations by suggesting that a young person has not had the benefit of child-rearing experiences that would have helped him or her develop adequate capacities to cope with life situations and relate comfortably to other people. With respect to planning for the future, there is also reason to believe that the developmental deficiencies suggested by low *EA* and *T* = 0 are likely to persist in young people in the absence of some coping skills training and interpersonal guidance. Information about the apparent need for such interventions can assist the court in determining provisions and requirements to be included in its custody decision.

Evaluating Possible Experience of Trauma

In addition to appreciating information about the general adjustment level and certain personality characteristics of young people and their parents, courts handling custody cases will typically want to be made aware of any indications that a child or adolescent has been exposed to traumatizing experiences. As described in the DSM-IV-TR, traumatic stress reactions consist of some combination of (a) marked fearfulness, with particular concerns about being hurt or damaged by accidents or aggressive acts and with manifestations in excessive worrying, upsetting recollections (flashbacks), and nightmares; (b) emotional and behavioral constriction, with shutting down of feelings (numbing), defensive avoidance of situations (withdrawal), and loss of interest in previously enjoyed activities; and (c) hyperarousal, as reflected in anxiety, irritability, difficulty concentrating, susceptibility to being startled, and heightened alertness to possible sources of danger in the environment (hypervigilance) (American Psychiatric Association, 2000).

Each of these features of traumatic stress reactions commonly gives rise to certain types of Rorschach responses. Marked fearfulness of bodily harm is suggested by an elevation on the Trauma Content Index (TCI $\geq$ .30) developed by Armstrong (1991, 2002), which is calculated by dividing the number of Aggressive (Ag), Sex (Sx), Morbid (MOR), Blood (Bl), and Anatomy (An) contents in a record by the total number of responses (R). Preoccupation with worrisome thoughts and recollections is suggested on the RIM when $FM + m > 6$ (an indicator of intrusive ideation) and $m > 2$ (an indicator of feeling helpless in the face of forces outside of one's control).

Constriction is measured on the RIM by an elevated Lambda (> .99) in a record of at least average length ($R > 16$), which reflects a narrow frame of reference and a preference for dealing with situations in a detached and simplistic manner without investing much thought or affect in them. Emotional constriction in particular is likely to be indicated by a $WSumC < 2.5$, which suggests a limited capacity to experience or express feelings; a $SumC' > WSumC$, which often identifies suppression of painful underlying affects that are being kept inside; and a low Affective Ratio ($Afr < .40$ or $< .50$, depending on EB style), which typically signifies avoidance of emotionally arousing situations.

Hyperarousal is indicated on the RIM by minus *D-scores*, which usually reveal a state of subjectively felt distress in which people are experiencing more demands than they can manage effectively. A combination of $D < -1$ with $AdjD \geq 0$ is likely to indicate substantial acute or situational stress, and $D < -1$ combined with $AdjD < -1$ points to a substantial and persistent stress overload. Hypervigilance is identified by a positive Hypervigilance Index (HVI), which suggests a cautious, mistrustful approach to people and events, preferably at a distance rather than up close. Further information about these and other Rorschach variables commonly associated with traumatic stress disorder is provided by Armstrong and Kaser-Boyd (2004), Holaday (2000), Luxenberg and Levin (2004), Sloan, Arsenault, and Hilsenroth (2002), and Sloan, Arsenault, Hilsenroth, Handler, and Harvill (1996).

Two important considerations govern the application of these and other Rorschach data in evaluating possible traumatic stress in the individual case. First, the absence of Rorschach indices of fearfulness and hyperarousal does not rule out the possibility that a person has experienced traumatic stress. This interpretive caution is particularly likely to apply when the type of defensive avoidance that leads to constriction in persons with stress disorder curtails their giving responses that would identify fearfulness and hyperarousal. In such instances, defensive avoidance can result in a bland and guarded Rorschach protocol that shows constriction but reveals little if any distress, despite evidence from other sources that the respondent has in fact developed a traumatic stress reaction.

Even with a list of group-validated Rorschach indices of traumatic stress, then, examiners cannot proceed properly without being well-grounded in the complexities of interpreting these indices in the context of interacting variables in a test protocol and in light of information from other tests and from a respondent's case history. Together with this consideration, the second important matter to keep in mind is the fact that neither fearfulness, constriction, nor hyperarousal (or any of the Rorschach indices associated with them) is specific to the experience of traumatic stress. Fearfulness is common among phobic persons, constriction among depressed individuals, and hyperarousal among young people and adults with a variety of anxiety disorders, to name just a few possible alternative explanations for why a child or adolescent might show Rorschach findings sometimes associated with stress disorder.

It is because most Rorschach variables neither rule out nor are specific to any one condition or previous life event that the RIM should not be used as the sole basis for deriving conclusions about particular conditions or events. Only when interpreted as part of a multi-faceted test battery and considered in the context of case history information can Rorschach findings about personality characteristics contribute their full measure of utility in facilitating clinical and forensic decision-making. The RIM shares this limitation with other personality assessment instruments, none of which can by itself provide definitive conclusions about what people have experienced or how they are likely to behave. All personality measures, whether performance-based or self-report in nature, work best as components of an integrative assessment that combines data from varied sources and determines the implications of these data in light of a respondent's life circumstances and sociocultural context. The scientific foundations and clinical utility of integrative personality assessment are elaborated by Beutler and Groth-Marnat (2003), Meyer (1997a), and Weiner (2003b, 2005).

Evaluating the Likelihood of Sexual Abuse

Just as there is no one personality profile that describes a "good" parent, there is no single set of personality characteristics that identifies whether a child has been sexually abused. Beginning with Browne and Finkelhor (1986) and continuing to the present time, reviews of research have indicated that the experience of having been sexually abused can lead to a variety of psychological outcomes (Kendall-Tackett, Williams, & Finkelhor, 1993, 2001; Merrill, Thomsen, Sinclair, Gold, & Milner, 2001; Rind, Tromovitch, & Bauserman, 1998; Sbraga & O'Donohue, 2003). These outcomes vary with the nature and circumstances of the abuse (e.g., at what age and persisting over what period of time, the prior relationship to the abuser, the extent to which the abuse was physical as well as sexual), and these outcomes include (but are not limited to) stress disorder, depression, sexual or interpersonal aversiveness, hypersexuality or promiscuity, and even no detectable psychological maladjustment.

Because there is no specific personality profile associated with having been sexually abused, neither the RIM nor any other personality assessment instrument can provide definitive evidence that such abuse has probably occurred. To be sure, some of the previously mentioned Rorschach indices of fearfulness, constriction, and hyperarousal may suggest this possibility, and numerous morbid Sex responses in a young person's record may lend some weight to such a suggestion. Rorschach studies of sexually abused children have indeed shown that, as a group, these young people are more likely than their non-abused peers to show various patterns of cognitive, affective, behavioral, and interpersonal maladjustment (Kamphuis, Kugeares, & Finn, 2000; Kelly, 1999; Leavitt, 2000; Leifer, Shapiro, Martone, & Kassem, 1991).

However, neither these group differences nor any Rorschach findings are specific to having been a victim of sexual abuse, and each of them can emerge as a consequence of other kinds of experiences. Although Rorschach assessment can be helpful in clarifying the adjustment problems and treatment needs of sexually abused young people, knowledgeable researchers and clinicians concur that Rorschach findings cannot and do not identify whether a child has been abused (Kelly, 1999; Kuehnle, 1996, chap. 9; Meyer & Archer, 2001; Weiner, Spielberger, & Abeles, 2002).

At the most, then, the RIM may provide clues to distressing preoccupations with morbidity and sexuality and thereby prompt investigation of whether sexual abuse may have occurred. Under no circumstances, however, do Rorschach findings by themselves warrant an inference that such abuse has probably occurred. Like its limits with respect to specificity, the RIM shares with other assessment instruments this limited ability to serve as the sole basis for identifying what may or may not have happened at some previous time in a respondent's life (see Weiner, 2003c).

PSYCHOMETRIC SOUNDNESS

Abundant research findings have documented that the RIM is a psychometrically sound measuring instrument with good to excellent intercoder agreement, substantial retest reliability, and adequate validity when used for its intended purposes. Further strengthening the psychometric foundations of Rorschach assessment is the availability of the previously mentioned normative reference data for 600 nonpatient adults and 1,390 nonpatient children, adolescents, together with reference data for adult samples of 535 psychiatric outpatients, 279 patients hospitalized with major depressive disorder, and 328 patients hospitalized with a first admission for schizophrenia (Exner, 2001, Tables 13-42). The scientific respectability of the RIM and its widespread use satisfy prevailing standards for admissibility into evidence, and survey data indicate that Rorschach findings are rarely excluded from courtroom testimony.

Intercoder Agreement

Numerous studies have demonstrated good to excellent intercoder agreement for CS Rorschach variables, whether measured by percentage agreement or by more sophisticated statistics like kappa and intraclass correlation coefficients (ICC). In one recent study exemplifying this line of research, involving four different samples and 219 protocols containing 4,761 responses, Meyer et al. (2002) found a median ICC of .93 for intercoder agreement across 138 regularly occurring Rorschach variables, with 134 of these variables falling in the excellent range for chance-corrected agreement. In another recent study, Viglione and Taylor (2003) examined coder concurrence for 84 protocols with 1,732 responses and found a median ICC of .92 for 68 variables considered to be of central interpretive significance in the CS. Earlier meta-analytic reviews and studies with patient and nonpatient samples identified mean kappa coefficients ranging from .79 to .88 across various CS coding categories, which for kappa coefficients is generally regarded as being in the good to excellent range (Acklin, McDowell, Verschell, & Chan, 2000; Meyer, 1997b, 1997c; Viglione & Taylor, 2003).

Some critics of the RIM have argued that these laboratory studies of intercoder agreement do not demonstrate "field" reliability, that is, an adequate level of coding agreement among individuals in practice (Hunsley & Bailey, 1999; Lilienfeld, Wood, & Garb, 2000). However, data from one of the samples in the Meyer et al. (2002) study of intercoder reliability and from a study sample reported by McGrath et al. (in press) have provided field reliability data. In both of these samples, patient protocols that had initially been coded in clinical practice, without any anticipation of their becoming part of a research project, were later coded independently for research purposes. The obtained correlation coefficients for intercoder agreement were more than adequate in both samples to demonstrate the potential field reliability of the RIM.

Of further note in this regard, moreover, research findings indicate that coding errors in clinical settings can be reduced by conscientious recourse to detailed coding criteria and guidelines that are readily available in textbooks and workbooks (McGrath, 2003). Accordingly, instances in which assessors in the field code Rorschach responses inaccurately, and thereby fail to reach substantial agreement with each other, would seem more likely to reflect insufficient preparation and care on part of examiners than any inherent shortcoming of the instrument.

Reliability

Retest studies with both children and adults over intervals ranging from 7 days to 3 years have demonstrated substantial reliability for Rorschach summary scores and indices that are conceptualized as relating to trait characteristics, which include almost all of the CS variables (see Exner, 2003, chap. 11; Gronnerod, 2003; Viglione & Hilsenroth, 2001). In adults, the short- and long-term stability of most CS variables exceed .75, and 19 core variables with major interpretive significance have shown 1-year or 3-year retest correlations of .85 or higher. The only Rorschach summary scores that show low retest correlations, even over brief intervals, are a few variables and combinations of these variables that are conceptualized as situationally influenced state characteristics.

Children show stability coefficients similar to those of adults when retested over brief intervals. When retested over 2-year intervals between the ages of 8 and 16, young people fluctuate considerably in their Rorschach scores early on but then show steadily increasing long-term consistency as they grow older. The increasing long-term stability of Rorschach variables from age 8 to age 16 is consistent with the expected gradual consolidation of personality characteristics that occurs during the developmental years (Exner, Thomas, & Mason, 1986).

Rorschach critics have argued that the reliability of the instrument is yet to be demonstrated, because only a portion of the CS variables have been included in reports of retest studies (Garb, Wood, Nezworski, Grove, & Stejskal, 2001). However, Viglione and Hilsenroth (2001) have published an extensive summary of the Rorschach retest data that encompasses, either individually or within some combination, virtually all of the CS structural variables and thus provides a full set of reliability data. The currently available retest correlations for all regularly occurring Rorschach variables having interpretive significance for trait dimensions of personality compare favorably with the reliability data for other frequently used and highly regarded assessment instruments, including scales of the Wechsler Adult Intelligence Scale-III (WAIS-III) and the Minnesota Multiphasic Personality Inventory (MMPI).

Validity

In the most thorough study of Rorschach validity available in the literature, Hiller, Rosenthal, Bornstein, Berry, and Brunell-Neuleib (1999) conducted a meta-analysis based on a random sample of Rorschach and MMPI research studies published from 1977 to 1997 in which there was at least one external (i.e., nontest) variable and in which some reasonable basis had been posited for expecting associations between variables. Their analysis of 2,276 Rorschach protocols and 5,007 MMPI protocols indicated almost identical validity for the RIM and the MMPI. The unweighted mean validity coefficients were .29 for Rorschach variables and .30 for MMPI variables, and there is no significant difference between these two validity estimates. Hiller et al. concluded that the validity for both the RIM and the MMPI "is about as good as can be expected for personality tests" (p. 291) and that average effect sizes of both instruments warrant examiner confidence in using them for their intended purposes.

Rorschach critics have nevertheless argued that the validity data for the Rorschach are not sufficient to warrant its use (Lilienfeld, Wood, & Garb, 2000). If true, this assertion in light of the Hiller et al. (1999) findings would indicate that neither the MMPI nor any other currently available personality assessment instrument should be used by practicing psychologists. These critics have maintained that the Hiller et al. meta-analysis is flawed, which seems unlikely given the care with which it was conducted and the methodological sophistication of those who conducted it (see Rosenthal, Hiller, Bornstein, Berry, & Brunell-Neuleib, 2001). These same critics have pointed out that the RIM does not correlate well with the MMPI, while ignoring not only method differences between the instruments but also research showing that the RIM and MMPI correlate quite well when people respond to both instruments in an open and forthcoming manner, as opposed to being guarded and defensive on either or both (Meyer, 1997a). They have noted that the RIM does not correlate well with psychiatric diagnosis, which it is not designed or intended to do. They have not published or adduced any original research in which the RIM has failed to show validity in a properly conceived and adequately designed study.

ADMISSIBILITY INTO EVIDENCE

Pursuant to the Frye and Daubert standards and the Federal Rules of Evidence, expert witness testimony is ordinarily admitted into evidence if it is likely to help the trier-of-fact reach its decision and is based on scientifically reliable methods and principles that are generally accepted in the professional community (see Ewing, 2003; Hess, 1999). In each of these respects, Rorschach testimony satisfies the prevailing criteria for admissibility.

First, the frequency with which Rorschach testimony has in fact been welcomed in the courtroom bears witness to its usefulness in facilitating legal decisions. In a survey of almost 8,000 cases in which forensic psychologists offered the court Rorschach-based testimony, the appropriateness of the instrument was challenged in only six instances, and in only one of these instances was the testimony ruled inadmissible (Weiner, Exner, & Sciara, 1996). In 90% of the total number of 247 cases between 1945 and 1995 in which Rorschach evidence was presented to a federal court of appeals, neither the admissibility nor the import of Rorschach findings was questioned by either the appellant or the respondent (Meloy, Hansen, & Weiner, 1997). When the relevance and utility of the Rorschach method was challenged in these appellate cases, the criticisms of the Rorschach testimony were typically directed at the interpretation of the data, not the method itself.

Second, the frequency with which the Rorschach method is taught and used demonstrates its general acceptance in the professional community. Surveys of psychologists over the past 40 years have consistently shown substantial endorsement of Rorschach testing as a valuable skill to teach, learn, and practice (see Camara, Nathan, & Puente, 2000; Clemence & Handler, 2001; Stedman, Hatch, & Schoenfeld, 2000; Viglione & Hilsenroth, 2001). These surveys indicate that over 80% of clinical psychologists engaged in providing assessment services use the RIM in their work and believe that clinical students should be competent in Rorschach assessment; over 80% of graduate clinical psychology programs teach the RIM; and training directors in psychology internship centers report that the RIM is one of the three measures most frequently used in their test batteries (the other two being the Wechsler Adult Intelligence Scale [WAIS]/Wechsler Intelligence Scale for Children [WISC] and the Minnesota Multiphasic Personality Inventory [MMPI-2/MMPI-A]).

With specific respect to forensic practice, data collected from forensic psychologists by Ackerman and Ackerman (1997), Boccaccini and Brodsky (1999), and Borum and Grisso (1995) showed 30% using the RIM in evaluations of competency to stand trial, 32% in evaluations of criminal responsibility, 41% in evaluations of personal injury, and 48% in evaluations of adults involved in custody disputes. In more recent surveys, Bow, Quinnell, Zaroff, and Assemany (2002) found that nearly half of their respondents use the RIM in assessing parents in a custody case who raise allegations of sexual abuse (41%) or are alleged to have been a perpetrator of sexual abuse (40%), and Budd, Felix, Poindexter, Naik-Polan, and Sloss (2002) reported that over 90% of 134 young people evaluated psychologically in a juvenile court setting to help determine their need for protection had been given projective personality measures.

Third, the research reviewed earlier in this article has documented the psychometric soundness of the RIM with respect to its intercoder agreement, retest reliability, and validity for measuring personality characteristics. The scientific respectability that derives from these empirical data accounts in part for the almost universal frequency with which Rorschach testimony is in fact admitted into evidence without challenge. Nevertheless, authors unfamiliar with these empirical findings or choosing to ignore them have asserted that CS Rorschach assessment lacks sufficient relevance and reliability to provide an admissible basis for courtroom testimony (e.g., Grove & Barden, 1999; Lilienfeld et al., 2000). For further counterpoint to this unwarranted assertion, readers are referred to articles by Hilsenroth and Stricker (2004), McCann (1998, 2004), and Ritzler, Erard, and Pettigrew (2002) in which the authors elaborate the ways in which Rorschach assessment satisfies several specific criteria for admissibility, including being standardized, testable, valid, reliable, extensively peer-reviewed, associated with a reasonable error rate, accepted by a substantial scientific community, and relevant to a wide range of psycholegal issues.

UTILITY

Finally of note with respect to the utility of the RIM in custody cases are three general respects in which Rorschach assessment may provide valuable information in forensic evaluations. First, the quantified indices provided by the CS allow an expert witness to specify in numerical terms the extent to which certain personality characteristics or adjustment difficulties are present, such as a person's level of reality testing, degree of subjectively felt distress, and extent of interest in other people.

Second, because the relatively unstructured nature of the RIM limits respondents' awareness of what their percepts might signify, Rorschach responses as mentioned at the beginning of this article often reflect aspects of personality functioning that people do not recognize in themselves or are reluctant to reveal during an interview or on a self-report inventory. As a consequence, there may be instances in which Rorschach findings add incremental validity to a psychological assessment by identifying personality characteristics, adjustment problems, or troubling concerns that might have gone undetected had not the RIM been included in the test battery (Weiner, 1999).

Third, the indirect manner in which the RIM measures personality states and traits makes it difficult for respondents to manufacture a false impression of themselves. Respondents trying to look more disturbed or impaired than they actually are typically overdo their efforts to appear incapacitated in ways that are obvious to experienced examiners. Respondents attempting to deny or conceal psychological difficulties may succeed in keeping these difficulties hidden, but they usually do so in ways that identify their guardedness and call into question the reliability of the test data they have given. This sensitivity of the RIM to attempted impression management, together with its quantification of personality characteristics and its capacity to transcend a respondent's conscious awareness and intent, often generate forensically critical data that would not otherwise have become available.

CONCLUSION

The Rorschach Inkblot Method (RIM) is a personality assessment instrument applicable to persons age 5 and older that provides dependable information relevant to a variety of issues in forensic cases involving contested custody. This Rorschach information includes reliable indications of (a) the extent to which parents and their children may have serious psychological disturbance or adjustment difficulties, (b) the presence in adults of personality characteristics that are likely to foster or to impede effective and nurturant parenting, and (c) the likelihood in children that they have experienced traumatic events.

Along with its utility in custody cases as a source of these three kinds of information, the RIM has definite limitations as well. Like all personality assessment instruments, first of all, the RIM works best in identifying emotional problems not as a sole data source, but when it is applied as part of a multi-faceted test battery and interpreted in light of each respondent's current circumstances and sociocultural context. With respect to personality characteristics, secondly, the implications of Rorschach findings for quality of parenting may vary with the particular needs of the children in a custody case and should be determined accordingly. Third, relevant Rorschach indices of stress reactions can be helpful in suggesting the occurrence of traumatic experiences when they are elevated (i.e., there are relatively few false positives), but these indices provide no basis for ruling out traumatic stress reactions when they are not elevated (e.g., there are frequent false negatives). Moreover, even when the experience of traumatic stress is suggested by Rorschach findings, there is no established basis for inferring that this stress resulted from having been sexually abused. All knowledgeable Rorschach scholars and clinicians concur that Rorschach assessment cannot and should not be used as a sole basis for determining whether a child has been sexually abused.

With respect to the utilization of Rorschach assessment in forensic cases, surveys have indicated widespread use of the RIM in applied settings, and extensive research findings have documented its scientific respectability with respect to intercoder agreement, retest reliability, validity, and a large normative reference base. Accordingly, despite the assertions of some Rorschach critics who fail to acknowledge or appreciate the import of the available empirical evidence, there is good reason to expect Rorschach-based testimony to be admitted into evidence in the courtroom, whichever of the current prevailing standards for admissibility is applied. Survey data in fact confirm that, even though testimony based on Rorschach findings may be challenged in the courtroom, the Rorschach method itself is rarely attacked, and Rorschach-based testimony is hardly ever ruled inadmissible. Because of its indirect nature as a performance-based rather than self-report personality measure, finally, the RIM may prove particularly helpful in custody and other forensic cases by virtue of its relative resistance to malingering or deception and its potential for bringing out information that people are unable or reluctant to disclose in response to direct inquiry.

REFERENCES

Ackerman, M. J., & Ackerman, M. C. (1997). Custody evaluations in practice: A survey of experience professionals (revisited). *Professional Psychology, 28*, 137-145.

Acklin, M. W., McDowell, C. J., Verschell, M. S., & Chan, D. (2000). Interobserver agreement, intraobserver agreement, and the Rorschach Comprehensive System. *Journal of Personality Assessment, 74*, 15-57.

American Psychiatric Association. (2000). *Diagnostic and statistical manual of mental disorders: Text revision* (4th ed.). Washington, DC: Author.

Armstrong, J. (1991). The psychological organization of multiple personality disordered patients as revealed in psychological testing. *Psychiatric Clinics of North America, 14*, 533-546.

Armstrong, J. (2002). Deciphering the broken narrative of trauma: Signs of traumatic dissociation on the Rorschach. *Rorschachiana, 25*, 11-27.

Armstrong, J., & Kaser-Boyd, N. (2004). Projective assessment of psychological trauma. In M. Hersen (Ed.-in-Chief) & M. Hilsenroth & D. Segal (Vol. Eds.), *Comprehensive handbook of psychological assessment: Vol. 2. Objective and projective assessment of personality* (pp. 500-512). Hoboken, NJ: Wiley.

Beutler, L. E., & Groth-Marnat, G. (2003). *Integrative assessment of adult personality* (2nd ed.). New York: Guilford.

Boccaccini, M. T., & Brodsky, S. L. (1999). Diagnostic test usage by forensic psychologists in emotional injury cases. *Professional Psychology, 30,* 253-259.

Borum, R., & Grisso, T. (1995). Psychological test use in criminal forensic evaluations. *Professional Psychology, 26,* 465-473.

Bow, J. N., Quinnell, F. Z., Zaroff, M., & Assemany, A. (2002). Assessment of sexual abuse allegations in child custody cases. *Professional Psychology, 33,* 566-575.

Browne, A., & Finkelhor, D. (1986). Impact of child sexual abuse: A review of the research. *Psychological Bulletin, 99,* 66-77.

Budd, K. S., Felix, E. D., Poindexter, L. M., Naik-Polan, A. T., & Sloss, C. F. (2002). Clinical assessment of children in child protection cases: An empirical assessment. *Professional Psychology, 33,* 3-12.

Camara, W. J., Nathan, J. S., & Puente, A. E. (2000). Psychological test usage: Implication in professional psychology. *Professional Psychology, 31,* 141-154.

Clemence, A. J., & Handler, L. (2001). Psychological assessment on internship: A survey of training directors and their expectations for students. *Journal of Personality Assessment, 76,* 18-47.

Ewing, C. E. (2003). Expert testimony: Law and practice. In I. B. Weiner (Ed.-in-Chief) & A. M. Goldstein (Vol. Ed.), *Handbook of psychology: Vol. 11. Forensic psychology* (pp. 55-66). Hoboken, NJ: Wiley.

Exner, J. E., Jr., (2001). *A Rorschach workbook for the comprehensive system* (5th ed.). Asheville, NC: Rorschach Workshops.

Exner, J. E., Jr. (2002, September). *The new nonpatient sample: An update.* Paper presented at the International Congress of Rorschach and Projective Methods, Rome, Italy.

Exner, J. E., Jr. (2003). *The Rorschach: A comprehensive system. Vol. 1. Basic foundations and principles of interpretation* (4th ed.). Hoboken, NJ: Wiley.

Exner, J. E., Jr., Thomas, E. A., & Mason, B. (1985). Children's Rorschachs: Description and prediction. *Journal of Personality Assessment, 49,* 13-20.

Exner, J. E., Jr., & Weiner, I. B. (1995). *The Rorschach: A comprehensive system. Vol. 3. Assessment of children and adolescents* (2nd ed.). New York: Wiley.

Ganellen, R. J. (1996). Comparing the diagnostic efficiency of the MMPI, MCMI-II, and Rorschach: A review. *Journal of Personality Assessment, 67,* 219-243.

Garb, H. N., Wood, J. M., Nezworski, M. T., Grove, W. M., & Stejskal, W. J. (2001). Towards a resolution of the Rorschach controversy. *Psychological Assessment, 13,* 433-448.

Gronnerod, C. (2003). Temporal stability in the Rorschach method: A meta-analytic review. *Journal of Personality Assessment, 80,* 272-293.

Grove, W., & Barden, R. (1999). Protecting the integrity of the legal system: The admissibility of testimony from mental health experts under *Daubert/Kumho* analysis. *Psychology, Public Policy, and the Law, 5,* 224-242.

Hess, A. K. (1999). Serving as an expert witness. In A. K. Hess & I. B. Weiner (Eds.), *Handbook of forensic psychology* (2nd ed., pp. 521-555). New York: Wiley.

Hiller, J. B., Rosenthal, R., Bornstein, R. F., Berry, D. T. R., & Brunell-Neuleib, S. (1999). A comparative meta-analysis of Rorschach and MMPI validity. *Psychological Assessment, 11*, 278-296.

Hilsenroth, M. J., & Stricker, G. (2004). A consideration of challenges to psychological assessment instruments used in forensic settings: Rorschach as exemplary. *Journal of Personality Assessment, 83*, 141-152.

Holaday, M. (2000). Rorschach protocols from children and adolescents diagnosed with posttraumatic stress disorder. *Journal of Personality Assessment, 75*, 143-157.

Hunsley, J., & Bailey, J. M. (1999). The clinical utility of the Rorschach: Unfulfilled promises and an uncertain future. *Psychological Assessment, 11*, 266-277.

Kamphuis, J., Kugeares, S., & Finn, S. (2000). Rorschach correlates of sexual abuse: Trauma content and aggression indexes. *Journal of Personality Assessment, 75*, 212-224.

Kelly, F. D. (1999). *The psychological assessment of abused and traumatized children.* Mahwah, NJ: Lawrence Erlbaum Associates.

Kendall-Tacket, K. A., Williams, L. M., & Finkelhor, D. (1993). The impact of sexual abuse on children: A review and synthesis of recent empirical studies. *Psychological Bulletin, 113*, 164-180.

Kendall-Tacket, K. A., Williams, L. M., & Finkelhor, D. (2001). Impact of sexual abuse on children: A review and synthesis of recent empirical studies. In R. Bull (Ed.), *Children and the law: Essential readings* (pp. 31-76). Malden, ME: Blackwell.

Kuehnle, K. (1996). *Assessing allegations of child sexual abuse.* Sarasota, FL: Professional Resource Press.

Leavitt, F. (2000). Surviving roots of trauma: Prevalence of silent signs of sex abuse in patients who recover memories of childhood. *Journal of Personality Assessment, 74*, 311-323.

Leifer, M., Shapiro, J., Martone, M., & Kassem, L. (1991). Rorschach assessment of psychological functioning in sexually abused girls. *Journal of Personality Assessment, 56*, 14-28.

Lilienfeld, S. O., Wood, J. M., & Garb, H. N. (2000). The scientific status of projective techniques. *Psychological Science in the Public Interest, 1*, 27-66.

Luxenberg, T., & Levin, P. (2004). The role of the Rorschach in the assessment of treatment of trauma. In J. P. Wilson & T. M. Keane (Eds.), *Assessing psychological trauma and* PTSD (2nd ed., pp. 190-225). New York: Guilford.

McCann, J. T. (1998). Defending the Rorschach in court: An analysis of admissibility using legal and professional standards. *Journal of Personality Assessment, 70*, 125-144.

McCann, J. T. (2004). Projective assessment of personality in forensic settings. In M. Hersen (Ed.-in-Chief) & M. Hilsenroth & D. Segal (Vol. Eds.), *Comprehensive handbook of psychological assessment: Vol. 2. Objective and projective assessment of personality* (pp. 562-572). Hoboken, NJ: Wiley.

McGrath, R. E. (2003). Enhancing accuracy in observational test scoring: The Comprehensive System as a case example. *Journal of Personality Assessment, 81*, 104-110.

McGrath, R. E., Pogge, D. L., Stokes, J. M., Cragnolino, A., Zaccario, M., Hayman, J. et al. (in press). Field reliability of Comprehensive System scoring in an adolescent inpatient sample. *Assessment.*

Meloy, J. R., Hansen, T., & Weiner, I. B. (1997). Authority of the Rorschach: Legal citations in the past 50 years. *Journal of Personality Assessment, 69,* 53-62.

Merrill, L. L., Thomsen, C. J., Sinclair, B. B., Gold, S. R., & Milner, J. S. (2001). Predicting the impact of child sexual abuse on women: The role of abuse severity, parental support, and coping strategies. *Journal of Consulting and Clinical Psychology, 69,* 992-1006.

Meyer, G. J. (1997a). On the integration of personality assessment methods: The Rorschach and the MMPI-2. *Journal of Personality Assessment, 68,* 297-330.

Meyer, G. J. (1997b). Assessing reliability: Critical correlations for a critical examination of the Rorschach Comprehensive System. *Psychological Assessment, 9,* 480-489.

Meyer, G. J. (1997c). Thinking clearly about reliability: More critical correlations regarding the Rorschach Comprehensive System. *Psychological Assessment, 9,* 495-498.

Meyer, G. J. (2001). Evidence to correct misperceptions about Rorschach norms. *Clinical Psychology: Science and Practice, 8,* 389-396.

Meyer, G. J., & Archer, R. (2001). The hard science of Rorschach research: What do we know and where do we go? *Psychological Assessment, 13,* 486-502.

Meyer, G. J., Hilsenroth, M. J., Baxter, D., Exner, J. E., Jr., Fowler, C. J., Piers, C. C. et al. (2002). An examination of interrater reliability for scoring the Rorschach Comprehensive System in eight data sets. *Journal of Personality Assessment, 78,* 219-274.

Rind, B., Tromovitch, P., & Bauserman, R. (1998). A meta-analytic examination of assumed properties of child sexual abuse using college samples. *Psychological Bulletin, 124,* 22-53.

Ritzler, B., Erard, R., & Pettigrew, T. (2002). Protecting the integrity of Rorschach expert witnesses: A reply to Grove and Barden (1999) re: The admissibility of testimony under Daubert/Kumho analysis. *Psychology, Public Policy, and the Law, 8,* 201-215.

Rosenthal, R., Hiller, J. B., Bornstein, R. F., Berry, D. T. R., & Brunell-Neuleib, S. (2001). Meta-analytic methods, the Rorschach, and the MMPI. *Psychological Assessment, 13,* 449-451.

Sbraga, T. P., & O'Donohue, W. (2003). Post hoc reasoning in possible cases of child sexual abuse: Symptoms of inconclusive origins. *Clinical Psychology: Science and Practice, 10,* 320-334.

Sloan, P., Arsenault, L., & Hilsenroth, M. (2002). Use of the Rorschach in the assessment of war-related stress in military personnel. *Rorschachiana, 25,* 86-122.

Sloan, P., Arsenault, L., Hilsenroth, M., Handler, L., & Harvill, L. (1996). Rorschach measures of posttraumatic stress in Persian Gulf War veterans: A three-year follow-up study. *Journal of Personality Assessment, 66,* 54-64.

Stedman, J., Hatch, J., & Schoenfeld, L. (2000). Preinternship preparation in psychological testing and psychotherapy: What internship directors say they expect. *Professional Psychology, 31,* 321-326.

Viglione, D. J., & Hilsenroth, M. J. (2001). The Rorschach: Facts, fictions, and future. *Psychological Assessment, 11*, 251-265.

Viglione, D. J., & Taylor, N. (2003). Empirical support for interrater reliability of Rorschach Comprehensive System coding. *Journal of Clinical Psychology, 59*, 111-121.

Weiner, I. B. (1999). What the Rorschach can do for you: Incremental validity in clinical applications. *Assessment, 6*, 327-338.

Weiner, I. B. (2001). Considerations in collecting Rorschach reference data. *Journal of Personality Assessment, 77*, 122-127.

Weiner, I. B. (2003a). *Principles of Rorschach interpretation* (2nd ed.). Mahwah, NJ: Lawrence Erlbaum Associates.

Weiner, I. B. (2003b). The assessment process. In I. B. Weiner (Ed.-in-Chief) & J. R. Graham & J. A. Naglieri (Eds.), *Handbook of psychology: Vol. 10. Assessment psychology* (pp. 3-25). Hoboken, NJ: Wiley.

Weiner, I. B. (2003c). Prediction and postdiction in clinical decision making. *Clinical Psychology: Science and Practice, 10*, 335-338.

Weiner, I. B. (2004). *Rorschach interpretation assistance program: Forensic report (RIAP5 FE)*. Lutz, FL: Psychological Assessment Resources.

Weiner, I. B. (2005). Integrative personality assessment with self-report and performance-based measures. In S. Strack (Ed.), *Personality and psychopathology* (pp. 317- 331). Hoboken, NJ: Wiley.

Weiner, I. B., Exner, J. E., Jr., & Sciara, A. (1996). Is the Rorschach welcome in the courtroom? *Journal of Personality Assessment, 67*, 422-424.

Weiner, I. B., Spielberger, C. D., & Abeles, N. (2002). Scientific psychology and the Rorschach Inkblot Method. *The Clinical Psychologist, 55*, 7-12.

Wood, J. M., Nezworski, M. T., Garb, H. N., & Lilienfeld, S. O. (2001). The misperception of psychopathology: Problems with the norms of the Comprehensive System of the Rorschach. *Clinical Psychology, 8*, 350-373.

Child Custody Evaluations in Cases Involving Sexual Abuse: A View from the Bench

The Honorable Debra K. Behnke
Mary Connell

SUMMARY. Psychological evaluation and testimony play a critical role in child sexual abuse cases, especially in custody and visitation cases. While the evaluation generally cannot determine whether sexual abuse has occurred, it can provide useful information to assist the court in deciding matters of custody and access in the face of the allegations. Judges need to know the standard of practice for the development of expert opinion in order to be able to evaluate testimony offered by custody evaluators. The informed judge can develop useful input by outlining expectations within the order for evaluation and actively regulating the gate for admission of expert testimony. Elements of a model order for

---

The Honorable Debra K. Behnke is the circuit judge in the 13th Judicial District in Florida. She has presided over a great number of family cases in her judicial career, and has a particular interest in contributing to the education of the judiciary regarding the use of expert testimony in disputed access cases with allegations of sexual abuse.

Mary Connell, EdD, is in independent practice in Fort Worth, Texas. A diplomate in forensic psychology, she provides training in child custody evaluation and evaluation involving allegations of sexual abuse in workshops sponsored by the American Academy of Forensic Psychology, of which organization she currently serves as president.

Address correspondence to Mary Connell (E-mail: mary@maryconnell.com).

[Haworth co-indexing entry note]: "Child Custody Evaluations in Cases Involving Sexual Abuse: A View from the Bench." Behnke, Debra K., and Mary Connell. Co-published simultaneously in *Journal of Child Custody* (The Haworth Press, Inc.) Vol. 2, No. 3, 2005, pp. 121-136; and: *Child Custody Litigation: Allegations of Child Sexual Abuse* (ed: Kathryn Kuehnle, and Leslie Drozd) The Haworth Press, Inc., 2005, pp. 121-136. Single or multiple copies of this article are available for a fee from The Haworth Document Delivery Service [1-800-HAWORTH, 9:00 a.m. - 5:00 p.m. (EST). E-mail address: docdelivery@haworthpress.com].

custody evaluations addressing allegations of sexual abuse are proposed. *[Article copies available for a fee from The Haworth Document Delivery Service: 1-800-HAWORTH. E-mail address: <docdelivery@haworthpress. com> Website: <http://www.HaworthPress.com> © 2005 by The Haworth Press, Inc. All rights reserved.]*

KEYWORDS. Sexual abuse, custody, judge, gatekeeper, expert testimony

In many jurisdictions, the judges assigned to the Family Court begin their tenure having had little or no judicial experience, and often no experience in the area of family law. There is little training given to judges in such highly specialized areas as familial sexual abuse, so they must heavily rely on expert testimony to make critical determinations when sexual abuse is alleged. Drawing upon years of experience as a judge hearing these matters, and with input from the perspective of the evaluator, we will offer a judicial view in considering expert testimony in child custody/sexual abuse matters.

HOW DOES EXPERTISE DEVELOP IN A CASE?

Mental health professionals or evaluators may become involved by way of court appointment, agreement between the parties, or retention by one party to a matter. When one party retains an expert for evaluation and testimony, the other party often follows suit. The use of experts by each party provides at least two points of view or opinion, potentially assisting the judge in deciding whether there is sufficient evidence of abuse to justify protective action, or in determining how to structure access to ensure that the child's safety and well-being are guarded. These experts' testimony should not be suspect simply because they are privately retained; it is proper, within the adversarial system, for litigants to present evidence, including expert testimony when appropriate, to support their claims or motions.

Nevertheless, courts may anticipate that experts chosen by a party have a built-in bias in favor of the party who retained them. The process of "building a case" against the other parent's wishes tends to focus attention on negative factors rather than on those issues about which there may be positive perceptions. The adversarial process and use of experts as advocates for each party may not serve the child's best interest in these and other respects.

Mental health professionals, and increasingly the courts, prefer that an expert be court-appointed (Ackerman & Ackerman, 1997; Bow, Quinnell, Zaroff, & Assemany, 2002; Champagne, Easterling, Shuman, Tomkins, & Whitaker, 2001). It has increasingly become the practice in family courts to identify a single expert to evaluate all parties, with equal access to the parties and opportunities to observe each parent in interaction with each child. This court-appointed evaluator, or evaluator mutually identified by the parties, is expected to be in a position to offer information that is balanced and free of bias. In reality, of course, the expert's personal biases may not be neutralized by this appointment or agreement of the parties; in matters so sensitive as sexual abuse of a child and so ambiguous as "the child's best interest," one's personal beliefs, biases, and emotions are often powerful competitors to actual data.

As does any forensic examiner, the mental health professional conducting the sexual abuse evaluation in the context of marital dissolution gathers information from many sources, attempts to resolve conflicting data, and eventually arrives at opinions or recommendations that might assist the court in the matter. The opinions or recommendations may embrace the ultimate issue before the court (Federal Rule of Evidence 704[1]) or may stop short of that, providing the court with useful information upon which the court can rely in making the determination. The evaluator may be able to offer no opinion, with a reasonable degree of psychological certainty, as to whether the alleged sexual abuse occurred. Likewise, it may be impossible for the court to make that determination with any degree of confidence. Nevertheless, the data gathered by the evaluator may illuminate aspects of alleged abuse in ways helpful to the court, and may result in other opinions helpful in managing the case. These may include related or peripheral recommendations, such as recommendations for further evaluation or treatment of the child or the parents, ways to structure access so that quality of contact is maintained without unduly compromising the child's safety and well-being, and ways to utilize alternative forms of dispute resolution to move the family forward. The evaluator provides findings and recommendations in a written report, and may subsequently be called to testify at a hearing.

GATEKEEPING FUNCTION OF THE JUDGE

There are certain evidentiary rules regarding admissibility of testimony as scientific evidence and in general, the testimony must meet standards of reliability and relevance in light of the matter before the court (*Daubert v. Merrell Dow Pharmaceuticals, Inc.*, 1993). In *Daubert*, the U.S. Supreme Court made trial judges "gatekeepers" who could apply broad discretion to determine whether or not scientific expert testimony was sufficiently reliable to be admitted. The *Daubert* court offered trial judges several factors, not intended to be exhaustive, to consider: whether the scientific theory or technique can be tested; whether it has been subjected to peer review; the size of the known error rate for findings; and whether the knowledge enjoys widespread acceptance in the scientific community (*Daubert*, pp. 593-594). Many states, however, do not consider psychological expert testimony on child sexual abuse to be "scientific evidence" as described by the *Daubert* court and thus subject to those rules governing admissibility.

The *Daubert* ruling left unresolved whether the court's gatekeeping function extended to expert testimony in applied science, technology, and other areas of specialized knowledge. In *Kumho Tire, Inc. v. Carmichael* (1999), the U.S. Supreme Court decided that, in accordance with Federal Rule of Evidence 702[2], a trial judge must determine whether expert testimony that "reflects scientific, technical or other specialized knowledge" has a "reliable basis in the knowledge and experience of [the relevant] discipline" (*Kumho*, p. 1174). Thus, whether the testimony of a child custody evaluator is regarded by the court as scientific or as "technical or other specialized knowledge," the court should exercise its gatekeeping function to establish reliability.

In addition to the admissibility of the opinion to be offered, there may be challenges to the qualifications of the expert to offer the opinion (FRE 702). In *re R.M. Children* (1995), the court addressed the way in which a trial judge should determine whether expertise has been sufficiently demonstrated to warrant admission of the testimony. In this case, the expert had a Bachelor of Arts in psychology, a Master of Science in occupational therapy, and a doctoral degree in clinical psychology. She had attended two daylong seminars specifically related to child sexual abuse. She also testified that she attended weekly supervisory sessions concerning sexual abuse with a supervisor whose training and experience she could not, in the court's opinion, adequately describe.

The Court found that, ". . . here, although Dr. X[3] holds a doctorate in clinical psychology and is licensed to practice that profession in New York state, her qualifications as a sexual abuse validator fall far short of what is required. Participation in two daylong seminars, by itself, is insufficient. That Dr. X previously qualified as an expert in family court, that she has received some additional supervision and that she has had some relevant experience during a relatively brief time span do not, without more, appreciably enhance her expertise."

In *Sharon B. W. v. George B. W.* (1998), the trial court did not qualify the proffered psychologist witness as an expert because he lacked significant experience with sexually abused children and had testified only a few times, but did allow him to testify as a lay witness. The appellate court described, citing *Gentry v. Mangum* (1995), a two-step inquiry in determining who is an expert:

> First, a circuit court must determine whether the proposed expert (a) meets the minimal educational or experiential qualifications (b) in a field that is relevant to the subject under investigation (c) which will assist the trier of fact. Second, a circuit court must determine that the expert's area of expertise covers the particular opinion as to which the expert seeks to testify. (*Sharon B. W. v. George B. W.*, p. 536)

The appellate court observed that the number of times the psychologist had testified was potentially relevant, but certainly not dispositive, of whether he should have been allowed to offer expert testimony, and since the expert met the minimum educational and experiential requirements, it was abuse of discretion to fail to qualify him as an expert. His testimony would have assisted the trier of fact. The appellate court did not, however, reverse the lower court's ruling, because the witness had in fact been permitted to testify.

Determining what weight to assign to expert testimony in child sexual abuse cases is frequently more difficult than determining the qualifications of the expert or the admissibility of the testimony, as evidenced in *In re Eli* (1993). In this case regarding overnight visitation for a father who was alleged to have sexually abused his child, the court engaged in a lengthy and instructive discussion regarding how a court should determine what weight to give an expert's testimony. This court set out specifically what evidence was presented by each of the mental health experts to support their opinions, what weight the court gave to each aspect of the experts' testimony, and the rationale for assignment of weight. Four experts, two psychologists and two social workers, testified. The court observed by illustration the basis for excluding expert testimony regarding culpability, noting that a four-year-old child treated at an emergency room for a slash wound to her shoulder, for example, might report to the physician that her father cut her with a razor. The doctor could testify that the slash wound was consistent with that allegation, but could not speak to the father's culpability. Likewise, a mental health expert may testify regarding what a child has said, and may opine about whether the child's diagnosis or mental illness was consistent with alleged sexual abuse, but could not testify about the culpability of the alleged sexual abuser. The "validator" who offers testimony regarding what an earlier witness has said, to buttress that witness's in-court testimony, should not be allowed to give a personal opinion regarding whether witness's statements are accurate. The validator may attempt to bolster the credibility of the witness, but the validator may not testify as to whether the alleged event actually occurred, for that is a determination for the court to make.

Moving on from the admissibility requirement to an examination of the weight to give expert testimony, the *Eli* trial court noted that expert opinion normally derives from clinical experience, experimental data, epidemiological data, or a combination of these data sources. The clinical method (in-depth examination of the presentation of a small number of homogenous patients seen for evaluation and treatment to distill hypotheses regarding the clinical picture) is perhaps useful for treatment decisions, but in most cases is insufficiently reliable to form the basis of an expert's opinion, the court noted. The epidemiological method, examining base rate data for a phenomenon among a large number of subjects, produces useful data, but the most reliable source of information is generally thought to be the experimental method. Regarding the testimony offered in this matter, the court observed that one of the expert witnesses gave far more substantive and helpful testimony than the others. She possessed an encyclopedic knowledge of the experimental literature on sexual abuse, and was otherwise far more qualified in this specialized area than the other experts; further, her opinions were developed through a range of techniques, including multiple interviews of relevant parties, collateral contacts, document review, and psychological testing. Her neutrality as a court-appointed expert further increased the relative weight of her testimony.

Although a court may qualify an individual as an expert in a case involving child sexual abuse, there is abundant case law that allows a judge to reject the expert's testimony. In *State v. MS* (1993), the Court stated:

> It is clear from the record that the trial court made a careful and studied review of all the relevant factors and that its determination awarding custody of the child to its mother is justified by the evidence. The court, as the trier of fact, was free to reject the testimony of the second court-appointed psychiatrist and of the experts retained by the petitioner and to credit the testimony of experts who testified on behalf of the respondent.

In *State v. Cressey* (1993), the Court discussed how "the determination of whether particular expert witness testimony is reliable and admissible, rests, in first instance, within the discretion of the trial court." In this case, the Court rejected the expert's testimony. Although the case involved criminal prosecution of child sexual abuse allegations, the court's in-depth discussion provides a useful framework for analyzing the reliability of expert testimony.

The prosecution offered an expert witness who would, if allowed, testify that the children exhibited symptoms consistent with those of sexually abused children (*State v. Cressey*, p. 696). In scrutinizing the methods relied upon by the expert to develop this opinion, the appellate court determined that the expert relied on several sources of information, including interviews of the children, a dissociative events scale to identify and assess any behaviors of the children that might be interpreted as manifestations of dissociative behavior resulting from post-traumatic stress, and an evaluation of the children through art therapy. The expert had asked the children to do a standard series of drawings to reveal their unconscious psychological processes. They had been asked to draw a person, then to draw a person of the opposite sex, and then a picture of the child's family. Last, they had been asked to draw themselves before, during, and after the abuse. The expert's analysis of these drawings was that several factors were potentially indicative of abuse. Cited as potentially relevant by the expert were the observations that the child first drew a person of the opposite sex, drew people with no secondary sex characteristics, and drew people with no hands, feet, or arms but with genitals.

The appellate court reversed and remanded the case back to the trial court, rejecting the state's contention that the expert's testimony was limited by statements that the children exhibited symptoms consistent with those of sexually abused children. Rather, the appellate court found that the jury could not distinguish between the expert proffering that the children's symptoms were consistent with sexual abuse and the expert blatantly opining the existence of sexual abuse. The risk that the jury would interpret the expert testimony as evidence of actual abuse was too great; thus, this court placed a limitation on admission of expert testimony.

The court further observed that expert psychological evidence can only be admissible if based at least partially on factors in addition to and independent of the child's account or statement. Otherwise, the expert's testimony is not new evidence but is merely vouching for the child's credibility. The court found that the expert could not have reached the opinions asserted based on those secondary factors, and noted the expert conceded this. Examining the secondary factors on which the expert relied to determine their reliability, the court noted that symptoms such as nightmares, forgetfulness, and overeating could just as easily be indicative of other problems as of sexual abuse, or might in fact just be normal developmental occurrences. The court noted an absence of standardized tests and quantifiable results. Without a more accurate means of assessing the implications of the symptoms exhibited by the children, the reliability of the expert's evaluation was questionable.

The court further noted that though symptoms may indeed be vague and inconsistent from case to case, this does not necessarily preclude their leading to a certain conclusion. In this case, there was no recognizable, logical nexus between many of the identified symptoms and the expert's conclusions that the children had been sexually abused. One child, for example, reportedly exhibited dissociative behavior suggestive of post-traumatic stress, but notably, had suffered the traumatic deaths of her mother and her aunt and the institutionalization of her father. Thus, to attribute these reported symptoms to alleged sexual abuse appeared, in the court's view, to lack merit.

Additionally, many of the behaviors cited appeared to the court to not only fail the reliability test, but to fail to even suggest that there was anything wrong with the child. "The fact that the children drew pictures of males when asked to draw a person does not put in motion any logical series of deductions that leads to a conclusion that the children were sexually abused," the court observed (*State v. Cressey*, 1993, p. 6). The court was not convinced that cross examination would be effective in exposing the unreliable elements that might underlie such expert testimony, and noted that the expert could easily dismiss any critique of the inconsistencies or potential shortcomings of individual pieces of the data, arguing that the evaluation relied on no one symptom or indicator, but that the opinion held true in light of all available factors and the expertise to interpret them. Thus, the court found that testimony would potentially be more prejudicial than probative. The court observed that this expert also relied on other data, such as the children's age-inappropriate sexual behavior and knowledge and obsessions with sexual abuse, factors that might indeed have been quite probative of whether sexual abuse had occurred. However, these factors were still not seen as a sufficient basis for an expert to affirmatively state that a child had been sexually abused. The reliability of the information upon which the expert formed his opinion was thus found to be questionable. A court may not rely on questionable evidence to determine guilt or innocence. The court noted that the expert might have served a useful function, educating the jury about delayed disclosure and inconsistencies in the children's reports, but that testimony could not be used to prove that a particular child had been sexually abused.

When there is little evidence of abuse, and the alleged victim is very young, is unable to testify, or gives inconsistent accounts, the battle of the experts can be problematic. Often a case may be decided based largely on whose expert is more believable or persuasive. In *Karen B. v. Clyde M.* (1991), a New York court observed, ". . . a dilemma that often confronts a judge, i.e., experts have rendered diametrically opposing opinions. The consequences of this court's decision to the child are potentially enormous. If she is placed with her mother, and the father is limited or excluded from having contact with her, when in fact he has done no harm, then a tremendous injustice results. If custody is placed with the father, and he has sexually abused her, an equal injustice with a potential for future harm ensues" (p. 270). The judge must carefully weigh the underlying data that support each expert's opinion, and take from the expert that which is relevant and reliable, recognizing that neither the expert nor the court may be able to ascertain whether or not abuse has thus far occurred. Family court judges should keep in mind that there are many reasons why genuine child sexual abuse may begin or first be disclosed at divorce, and why a person undergoing a divorce may make a good faith but mistaken allegation. False allegations may, of course, be based upon overinterpretation or misinterpretation of events and symptoms, or, more rarely, may be deliberately contrived (Faller, 1991). Although deliberately fabricated allegations may be made to influence the custody decision or to hurt an ex-spouse, knowledgeable professionals view these as infrequent events and it is critical that every allegation be treated with the utmost seriousness.

Judges can reasonably expect that custody evaluators will be familiar with and will adhere to the professional standards and guidelines that inform competent practice in their areas of specialization, and will be able to demonstrate, when testifying, the relevant competencies in knowledge, training and experience required for such work. The psychologist who does custody evaluations is directed by ethical standards (Ethical Principles of Psychologists and Code of Conduct, American Psychological Association, 2002), professional guidelines (Guidelines for Child Custody Evaluations in Divorce Proceedings, American Psychological Association, 1994; Specialty Guidelines for Forensic Psychologists, Committee on Ethical Guidelines for Forensic Psychologists, 1991; and Model Standards of Practice for Child Custody Evaluations, Association of Family and Conciliation Courts, undated), and state psychology board rules of practice that govern or guide psychologists in general, and child custody evaluators specifically, in developing relevant competencies and conducting adequate custody evaluations.

In summary, then, the court should take an active role in determining whether the proffered expert testimony rests on a foundation sufficiently reliable and relevant to the matter at hand to justify its admission. The expert's knowledge, training, and experience must be determined to be sufficiently relevant to the expertise required for the opinion to be offered. The opinion should derive from multiple data sources, each independently bearing some demonstrably logical and reliable connection to the matter about which an opinion is to be offered. The expert should be able to distinguish between empirically supported opinion (that which the court will admit) and more general clinical impressions, which the court may determine lack sufficient reliability to merit consideration. Whether these more general clinical impressions are more probative than prejudicial remains a matter of some controversy, and the court must rely upon evidence presented to make that determination. Data that might bear consideration by the court include evidence of the expert's objectivity or neutrality in giving equal consideration to rival hypotheses, in searching out data that would support or refute each line of reasoning on the matter, and in guarding against overstatements of certainty.

A MODEL ORDER FOR CUSTODY EVALUATION IN SEXUAL ABUSE MATTERS

In order to ensure that the court conveys to the evaluator the expectation of a thorough, balanced, and wide-reaching assessment, the court may wish to consider an order including most or all of the following elements, adapted to meet the needs of a particular case. The model order, drawn from elements in the guidelines and in professional publications (APA, 1994; AFCC, 1994; Bow, Quinnel, Zaroff, & Assemany, 2002; Kuehnle, 2002; Kuehnle, 1996), might identify:

1. The range of information to be reviewed by the evaluator, for example:
   a. the Child Protective Services file; the police reports and witness statements;
   b. the child's school records, including anecdotal notes of behavioral issues, the child's medical records from birth to the present time, and the child's psychotherapy records;
   c. the alleged perpetrator's criminal history information; driving record; medical records; psychotherapy records; police records, including any records of domestic disturbance calls to the party's home or any previous residence of the alleged perpetrator; and prior CPS records;
   d. the other parent's prior legal records or police reports; prior CPS records; and psychotherapy records;
   e. and any other documents the evaluator requests.
2. The parties to be included in the assessment, for example:
   a. The evaluator is to complete a full assessment of each party and the child, and
   b. A full evaluation or interviews with each step-parent or involved grandparent, at the evaluator's discretion.
3. The nature and rough approximation of number of times of contact, for example:
   a. The evaluator should conduct multiple interview/testing sessions with each adult party, alternating the adults, and should consider the efficacy of accomplishing a significant portion of these activities before meeting the child. This may provide some enrichment of the examiner's awareness of relevant factors potentially influencing the parents' presentation, and of the concerns of the parents regarding the examiner's upcoming contact with the child. The examiner may consider the importance of completing most or all of the interviews and testing of the parents before meeting the child;
   b. The evaluator will have opportunities to observe each parent with the child in the evaluator's office, the parent's home, or another location; observation sessions will occur at the evalu-

ator's discretion and should alternate between the parents. When there has been a period of no contact between the accused parent and the child, the evaluator may elect to observe the first encounter, or may elect to schedule the observations of the child after there have been opportunities for restored contact, through supervised visitation if necessary. The evaluator develops a plan for observations during the course of the custody evaluation, and conveys this plan to the parties directly or through their counsel. Attorneys will cooperate (barring objections to be considered by the court) with the evaluator's requests in arranging the observations, providing a means, if requested by the evaluator, for each parent to have a significant period of contact with the child prior to observation(s) (supervised, if necessary, by a neutral supervisor, such as the guardian ad litem or a professional supervisor);

c. The evaluator will have the opportunity for telephone or in-person interviews with collateral sources of information, to be determined by the evaluator (recommended to include, at a minimum, pediatricians who have examined or treated the child, the child's therapist, the CPS investigator, the Crimes Against Children investigator, the child's teachers, and the child's substitute caregivers).

4. Working agreement between the court and the court-appointed evaluator. For example:

a. The evaluator has discretion regarding psychological testing to be utilized, but is encouraged to rely upon instruments with demonstrated reliability and validity for providing information useful and relevant to the current psycholegal question. It is understood that the results of testing may, at best, generate hypotheses that the evaluator and the court may find useful in developing recommendations or plans for ensuring the child's well-being and safety and the child's best interests.

b. Should the evaluator lack expertise in interviewing children for whom there is suspicion of child sexual abuse, assessing alleged perpetrators of sexual abuse of children, or assessing any other matters at issue in this case, it is expected that the evaluator will:

   i. make known this limitation, and

   ii. refer the portion of the assessment for which experience is lacking to an experienced evaluator, or

        iii. obtain consultation sufficient to assist the evaluator in doing an adequate assessment.

c. The court does not expect the evaluator to determine whether the alleged sexual abuse occurred; that is a matter for the court to determine. The court seeks the evaluator's opinion about:

    i. the relative strength of support for the finding that abuse occurred,

    ii. and all considerations that raise doubt

    iii. based on:

        1. the relevant literature regarding base rates of sexualized behavior and other acting out for children of this age and for children whose parents are divorcing;

        2. interview or questioning techniques that may have affected the child's statements;

        3. and other issues that may have raised concern on the part of the accusing parent.

d. The court seeks a careful examination of all of the relevant history, chronology of events, application of the research to the data available in this case, and an informed opinion about data that tend to support and data that tend to refute the notion that sexual abuse has occurred.

e. By agreeing to accept the appointment, the evaluator agrees to provide an assessment that essentially comports with these parameters. If it is the evaluator's opinion that substantial change in this order must be made in order to allow the evaluator to maintain an appropriate standard of practice:

    i. The appointed evaluator should notify the court, in writing, of the recommended changes before proceeding with the evaluation.

    ii. When the court has reviewed the proposed changes, the evaluator will be informed whether the court is modifying the order to embrace the recommended changes or withdrawing the appointment.

    iii. If, during the conduct of the assessment, the evaluator determines that a change in procedures, in variance with the order, is clinically or forensically indicated, then the evaluator should proceed with the change in procedures and complete the assessment, including in the written report an explanation for the change.

RATIONALE

The adoption of a detailed order such as the one proposed above may serve several functions. It may assist the court in formulating a clear expectation of what the evaluator can reasonably contribute to the determinations that must be made. Both the judge and the attorneys may benefit from the reminder that there are limits to psychological expertise, and that the evaluator possesses no techniques that are dispositive of sexual abuse, an external event that may or may not have occurred to a particular child by a specific perpetrator (Kuehnle, 1996). Second, the detailed order may assist the parties in anticipating the range of the exploration that should be included in the assessment. Third, the detailed order may assist the novice evaluator in appreciating the specialized nature of the assessment to be undertaken, and may support the more experienced evaluator to fashion an assessment that will, indeed, meet the needs of the court. While the evaluator is ultimately responsible for determining procedures to be utilized in any professional service to be provided, this detailed order makes it the responsibility of the evaluator who is unwilling to undertake such thorough assessment to decline the appointment. Minor changes in the nature of the evaluation to be undertaken can be proposed by the evaluator and endorsed by the court prior to the initiation of the assessment, or, if their need becomes apparent during the assessment, made at the evaluator's discretion, with an explanation proffered in the report. This procedure preserves the forensic clinician's freedom to determine the procedures to be utilized, in keeping with the court's general expectation for a thorough, balanced evaluation. Importantly, the parties are well served by clarity of purpose from the outset, so that important time, energy, and financial resources are not squandered on an assessment that is of limited utility to the process.

NOTES

1. Federal Rule of Evidence 704, Opinion on Ultimate Issue, holds that "(a) Except as provided in subdivision (b), testimony in the form of an opinion or inference otherwise admissible is not objectionable because it embraces an ultimate issue to be decided by the trier of fact. (c) No expert witness testifying with respect to the mental state or condition of a defendant in a criminal case may state an opinion or inference as to whether the defendant did or did not have the mental state or condition constituting an element of the crime charged or of a defense thereto. Such ultimate issues are matters for the trier of fact alone.

2. Federal Rule of Evidence 702, Testimony by Experts, holds that "If scientific, technical, or other specialized knowledge will assist the trier of fact to understand the evidence or to determine a fact in issue, a witness qualified as an expert by knowledge, skill, experience, training, or education, may testify thereto in the form of an opinion or otherwise, if (1) the testimony is based upon sufficient facts or data, (2) the testimony is the product of reliable principles and methods, and (3) the witness has applied the principles and methods reliably to the facts of the case."

3. The authors of this paper decided not to include the name of the psychologist mentioned in the court's opinion.

REFERENCES

Ackerman, M., & Ackerman, M. (1997). Custody evaluation practices: A survey of experienced professionals (Revisited). *Professional Psychology: Research and Practice, 28,* 137-145.

American Psychological Association (2002). Ethical principles of psychologists and code of conduct. *American Psychologist, 57,* 1060-1073.

American Psychological Association (1994). Guidelines for child custody evaluations in divorce proceedings. *American Psychologist, 49,* 677-680.

Association of Family and Conciliation Courts (undated). Model standards of practice for child custody evaluations. Milwaukee, WI: Author.

Bow, J. N., Quinnell, F. A., Zaroff, M., & Assemany, A. (2002). Assessment of sexual abuse allegations in child custody cases. *Professional Psychology: Research and Practice, 33,* 566-575.

Champagne, A., Easterling, D., Shuman, D. W., Tomkins, A. J., & Whitaker, E. (2001). Are court-appointed experts the solution to the problems of expert testimony? *Judicature, 84,* 178-183.

Committee on Ethical Guidelines for Forensic Psychologists (1991). Specialty guidelines for forensic psychologists. *Law and Human Behavior, 15* (6), 655-665.

Daubert v. Merrell Dow Pharmaceuticals, Inc., 509 U.S. 579 (1993).

Faller, K. C. (1991). Possible explanations for child sexual abuse allegations in divorce. *American Journal of Orthopsychiatry, 61,* 86-91.

Federal Rules of Evidence, Rule 702, 704 (2004).

Gentry v. Mangum, 195 W. Va. 512, 466 S.E.2d 171 (1995).

In re Eli, 607 N.Y.S. 2d 535 (N.Y. Fam. Ct. 1993).

In re R.M. Children, 627 N.Y.S. 2d 869 (N.Y. Fam. Ct. 1995).

Karen B. v. Clyde M., 574 N.Y.S. 2d 267 (N.Y. Fam. Ct. 1991).

Kuehnle, K. (1996). *Assessing allegations of child sexual abuse.* Sarasota, FL: Professional Resource Exchange, Inc.

Kuehnle, K. (2002). Child sexual abuse evaluations. In A. M. Goldstein & I. B. Weiner (Eds.) *Comprehensive handbook of psychology, volume eleven: Forensic psychology* (pp. 437-460). New York: Wiley & Sons.

Kumho Tire, Inc. v. Carmichael, 119 S.Ct.1167 (1999).

Nichols, H. R., & Molinder, I. (1999). *Psychosexual Life History Inventory.* Tacoma, WA: Nichols and Molinder Assessments.
Sharon B. W. v. George B. W., 507 S.E. 2d 401 (W.Va. 1998).
State v. Cressey, 628 A. 2d 696 (N.H. 1993).
State v. MS, 592 N.Y.S. 2d 708 (N.Y. Sup. Ct. 1993).
Truax v. Truax, 874 P. 2d 10 (Nev. 1994).
Wiederholt v. Fischer, 485 N.W. 2d 442 (Wis. Ct. App. 1992).

Index

BOOK ORDER FORM!

Order a copy of this book with this form or online at:
http://www.haworthpress.com/store/product.asp?sku= 5747

Child Custody Litigation
Allegations of Child Sexual Abuse

____ in softbound at $19.95 ISBN-13: 978-0-7890-3134-1 / ISBN-10: 0-7890-3134-5.
____ in hardbound at $39.95 ISBN-13: 978-0-7890-3133-4 / ISBN-10: 0-7890-3133-7.

COST OF BOOKS _____

POSTAGE & HANDLING _____
US: $4.00 for first book & $1.50
for each additional book
Outside US: $5.00 for first book
& $2.00 for each additional book.

SUBTOTAL _____

In Canada: add 7% GST. _____

STATE TAX _____
CA, IL, IN, MN, NJ, NY, OH, PA & SD residents
please add appropriate local sales tax.

FINAL TOTAL _____
If paying in Canadian funds, convert
using the current exchange rate,
UNESCO coupons welcome.

❏ **BILL ME LATER:**
Bill-me option is good on US/Canada/
Mexico orders only; not good to jobbers,
wholesalers, or subscription agencies.

❏ **Signature** _____

Payment Enclosed: $ _____

❏ **PLEASE CHARGE TO MY CREDIT CARD:**

❏ Visa ❏ MasterCard ❏ AmEx ❏ Discover
❏ Diner's Club ❏ Eurocard ❏ JCB

Account # _____

Exp Date _____

Signature _____
(Prices in US dollars and subject to change without notice.)

PLEASE PRINT ALL INFORMATION OR ATTACH YOUR BUSINESS CARD

Name

Address

City   State/Province   Zip/Postal Code

Country

Tel   Fax

May we use your e-mail address for confirmations and other types of information? ❏ Yes ❏ No We appreciate receiving
your e-mail address. Haworth would like to e-mail special discount offers to you, as a preferred customer.
We will never share, rent, or exchange your e-mail address. We regard such actions as an invasion of your privacy.

Order from your **local bookstore** or directly from
The Haworth Press, Inc. 10 Alice Street, Binghamton, New York 13904-1580 • USA
Call our toll-free number (1-800-429-6784) / Outside US/Canada: (607) 722-5857
Fax: 1-800-895-0582 / Outside US/Canada: (607) 771-0012
E-mail your order to us: orders@haworthpress.com

For orders outside US and Canada, you may wish to order through your local
sales representative, distributor, or bookseller.
For information, see http://haworthpress.com/distributors

(Discounts are available for individual orders in US and Canada only, not booksellers/distributors.)

Please photocopy this form for your personal use.
www.HaworthPress.com

BOF06